D1270308

A
Family
Matter

A Family Matter

A Parents' Guide to
Homosexuality
by
Dr. Charles Silverstein

McGraw-Hill Book Company
New York   St. Louis   San Francisco   London
Düsseldorf   Mexico   Panama   Toronto

Book design by Bob Mitchell.

123456789FGFG783210987

Library of Congress Cataloging in Publication Data

Silverstein, Charles.
A family matter.
Bibliography: p.
1. Homosexuality—United States.   2. Homosexuals—
United States—Family relationships.   I. Title.
HQ76.3.U5S56   301.42'7   77-4224
ISBN 0-07-057429-4

This book is dedicated
to my mother and father

CONTENTS

ACKNOWLEDGMENTS

Many people have contributed to this book. My experiences at the Institute for Human Identity motivated me to gather the material. My colleagues, particularly Bernice Goodman, have been instrumental in clarifying some of the ideas expressed here. William Bory worked many hours correcting the manuscript and offering good advice. Frank E. Taylor contributed his usual good advice and consultation throughout the preparation of this book. Finally, I need to acknowledge the warm reception I received from families who wanted their stories told. Hopefully I have done it well enough.

FOREWORD

This book is for families who want to learn how to deal with a homosexual son or daughter, and come to terms with their own feelings about homosexuality. As far as I know, this is the first book written by a professional (a practicing psychologist) especially for you, the family of a homosexual.

One purpose of the book is to help parents and children talk together. Talk can be used constructively or destructively. I'll be suggesting ways to make your family discussions constructive ones.

You also need information about what homosexuality is and what the lives of homosexuals are like. There are a number of chapters devoted to this. Since no one book can give all the information, I have included an annotated bibliography in the appendix.

I think it's a good idea for your children to read this book. Perhaps your child has given it to you after reading it himself. That would be ideal. Just as parents need to understand the problems of their homosexual children, so these children need to understand the problems of their parents.

The experiences of a number of families form the basis of the book. In each of these families one child is homosexual. All of the stories are true. All the events are taken from actual case histories, although each chapter is a composite of more than one family. Names and other identifying information have been changed to ensure anonymity. These stories were told to me by homosexual children and members of their families in the knowledge that they would be used in this book. These people shared their experience in the hope it would help other families. Without their experience as our guide, this book could not have been written.

Now, before you continue reading, let me make a suggestion. *Don't read this book in secret.* The first lesson in coping with homosexuality in a family is rejecting secrecy between the parents and the child. This means that you have to talk about homosexuality. It may be difficult at first, but, like most things, it gets easier as you go along. Speaking openly and honestly promotes a feeling of trust. This book is meant to help you achieve that goal.

Finally, I need to introduce a new word into your vocabulary. The word is "gay." In most parts of the United States homosexuals call themselves gay. This usage was originally confined to the homosexual, or gay, subculture, but now the word is increasingly understood in this sense by both heterosexuals and homosexuals.

Early in this century, when homosexuality was a well-hidden secret, "gay" was used as a code word by homosexuals. With the passage of time, it has gained general acceptance as a synonym for *homosexual.* Yet it signifies much more than that to gay people. For gay people, the word represents a new perception of themselves, a perception unencumbered by feelings of doubt and low self-esteem. For gays the word represents a place they have made for themselves in society. Since I believe that people have the right to designate themselves, I use the term throughout this book.

There's a good deal of special terminology in the gay world, and your son or daughter will be able to teach you a whole new set of terms. You'll find them quite vivid, though perhaps not always to your liking. An understanding of this vocabulary will be helpful in learning what homosexuality is about, and what it means to be gay.

A
Family
Matter

Information
for
Parents

chapter one

DANGER
OR OPPORTUNITY

I decided to write this book after Mrs. K., an intelligent woman of seventy, came to me for help. She entered my office looking sad and lonely. It was only with the greatest effort that she could tell the story that had caused her so much suffering. Speaking slowly, pausing as if to test my response, she began to tell me what was troubling her. Then, as she saw my interest, she spoke more quickly and clearly, until finally she started to cry. It was the first time she had told anyone about what had happened and what it meant to her.

She had recently called her thirty-five-year-old son, Michael. She was proud of Michael, a man who had worked diligently in his business and was now reaping the rewards of success. Michael had told Mrs. K. that he had been asked to appear on a national television program. Excited by the news, as most mothers would be, Mrs. K. asked what the program was about. Michael avoided answering her question and said that they could discuss it later. As Michael explained, he was to be interviewed in his own home and the interview would be broadcast later in the month. He invited his mother to come and watch the filming and said it would be a good idea to arrive well before the camera crew got there. She was thrilled by the invitation.

When Mrs. K. arrived, Michael greeted her warmly but somewhat nervously. He said it was important that they talk about the television program and why he was appearing. As they sat down on the couch, Mrs. K. saw the tension in Michael's face and knew that this was not to be an ordinary conversation.

Michael told her that he was a homosexual. He was appearing on the program as a representative of a gay liberation organization, to speak out for the abolition of laws against homosexuality. Mrs. K. was jolted by the news. She had never thought that Michael, who had always been popular with women, might be a homosexual. She began to cry. Then, just as suddenly, she stopped crying and looked at her son. For the first time in her life she wondered whether she knew the man who sat beside her. It was as if he were a foreign creature, a lookalike of her son. She could feel a small empty space beginning to form inside her. As she stared at Michael she thought of her husband, who had been dead for many years, and the space began to enlarge. She felt sad and very lonely.

The camera crew arrived early and Mrs. K. welcomed the interruption. She watched and listened to the interview, but she really didn't understand any of the things Michael said. Mrs. K. knew nothing of homosexuality, and her personal discomfort precluded any consideration of the civil rights issues being discussed. She was thinking only of her son.

Mrs. K. felt even worse when the program went on the air. Perhaps other members of her family would be watching that night. Friends or neighbors might be watching, people who knew her and her son. She felt profoundly embarrassed.

She wanted to talk to Michael, but not knowing what to say to him or what questions to ask made her feel ignorant. She decided to educate herself and looked for a book addressed to people in her situation. When that search failed, she decided to find a person who could educate her. Since she couldn't talk to relatives, Mrs. K. began to ask her friends about homosexuality, pretending that the information was for someone else. She quickly learned that they also were poorly informed. It was bad enough, Mrs. K. thought, that her son was a homosexual (whatever that meant), but what was even worse, she couldn't find any reliable information for parents who discover homosexuality in their families. More than anything else, her lack of knowledge made her feel frustrated and helpless.

Mrs. K. turned to me, a psychologist who has specialized in working with gay people. She hoped I could give her some information about homosexuality and some insights to aid her in understanding her son.

As I listened to this woman I realized how difficult her life must have been in the three months since her son's disclosure. In all probability she had grown up at a time when discussion of any kind of sexuality, much less homosexuality, was unheard of. All of us, to a greater or lesser extent, were brought up in similar circumstances, and our knowledge of the various forms of sexual expression is severely limited.

Mrs. K., a very sane and cultivated woman, advanced the idea that there must be a great conspiracy to hide information about homosexuality. She asked me why we psychologists hadn't written books for parents like her. "Why are you always writing books to help the children? Don't you think we parents need help too?"

I knew there was nothing available anywhere that was directly aimed at helping parents or relatives of a homosexual man or woman. Although the literature about homosexuality is enormous, none of it offers clear, useful information for the family.

After the discussion with Mrs. K., I began to think about how many other Mrs. K.'s there must be in the world. Parents, brothers and sisters, grandparents, friends—people who want to understand someone they love. They have all been ignored. The little bits of information they might glean from popular or even scientific articles were usually inaccurate and often negative.

This book is dedicated to people like Mrs. K.—and to people like you who believe in family unity. My experience is that families want to resolve their problems, and I think the proper role for a psychologist is helping them do it. I know that having a gay child can precipitate a crisis in your family. I also know that a family crisis can be resolved when family members love each other and desire its resolution.

The family is an important institution, though it has been considerably weakened in the modern world. Some people even think that the family as an institution is dead. I don't believe so. I think the family is still the most important structure in our lives, and that its primary role is the mutual support of its members. The family has to care about itself, not the outside world. Parents and children need to see each other as individuals, each with needs of his or her own, and they should help each other fulfill those needs. In a world where values are changing at breakneck speed, the family should be a place where people can slow down a bit and consider how these changing values are affecting them. The family also must be willing to change its own values from time to time. That's the hardest part.

By growing and developing their own values, every son and daughter will change the family in some important ways. If families can develop techniques for adapting to the changing styles of their members, they will insure the usefulness of the family and guarantee the pleasure and security that only it can provide.

There is no question that many families must change when they learn that a son or daughter is gay. The question is, will the changes make the family stronger and lead its members to a closer and more honest relationship, or will they generate the sort of conflict that scars family members for the rest of their lives?

Being a parent is the toughest job in the world. Like most parents, you've probably made many personal and financial sacrifices for your children. No one ever guaranteed that you'd receive commensurate emotional benefits in return—and there's certainly no retirement plan for parents. Although you had no training, everyone expects you to do the job perfectly. If the kids accomplish good things in their lives, they get the credit. If they turn out to be a disappointment, you get the blame.

Parents are told to let their children live their own lives. Your children have the freedom to choose their friends, choose their occupations, make and spend money the way they like, have sex whenever and with whomever they choose, and you know only what they want you to know. And what if they make serious mistakes? You get the blame, even if it comes from no one but yourself.

Why are parents held responsible for the errors of their children? It's embarrassing for a psychologist to admit it, but the professions of psychology and psychiatry have misled us into believing that parents are responsible for the actions of their children. In the first part of this century psychological theories were poured liberally into the American home, and all the conflicts and neurotic problems of the children were held traceable to the neurotic problems of their parents. Children were usually pictured as passive recipients of the parents' values. It was as if children were unformed lumps of clay, with no values or temperament of their own.

Nowhere has this unfortunate, and inaccurate, idea done more harm than in families such as yours. Guilt is the universal reaction of parents when they find out that they have raised a child who has become a homosexual. They feel guilty because they have been taught to see homosexuality in a negative light and to hold themselves responsible for their children's behavior. The old psychological theories treated homosexuality as a "mental disorder" created by the parents. The effect was to make homosexual people feel that they were mentally ill, and make parents feel that they had destroyed the lives of the people they loved most, their children.

But times have changed, and so have the theories. Psychologists and psychiatrists have investigated the lives of homosexuals much more carefully in the past twenty years, and most of us now believe that homosexuality is not an illness. Later we'll discuss this issue in more detail.

Psychologists have learned more about family communication too. We've learned how some families create an atmosphere of solidarity and how others destroy themselves through conflict. Our experience with family therapy has shown us how families can work together to resolve crisis.

A gay person's family is very important. Some people believe that a child's homosexuality represents a rejection of the family. Some people even believe that homosexuality per se is a threat to the family, as if it were intrinsically inimical to the idea of family life.

Nothing could be further from the truth. Homosexuals need to be part of their families as much as any other children. Perhaps more so, since most gay people do not marry and raise families of their own. Given the opportunity, they prefer to remain loyal to their own parents and relatives. In our society the homosexual is likely to be attacked for his or her sexual preference by friends, employers, police and much of organized religion. The family is one place where a gay person most needs to feel accepted. They hope their parents, the people who know them best, will see that they're the same persons they've always been.

A gay man wants his parents to see him as their son, not their homosexual son. Either that son is a loving person to his parents and brothers and sisters and a useful and productive person in society, or he is not. His homosexuality has nothing to do with it. Sexual preference has nothing to do with character. It has nothing to do with social abilities or intelligence. It has nothing to do with the capacity to love and show affection. It has nothing to do with a sense of honesty. The only way in which a homosexual person differs from a heterosexual person is in sexual preference.

One of the most destructive things a parent can do is overemphasize a family member's homosexuality. If you treat him only as "my homosexual son" you will force him to experience in his home the same discomfort he experiences in the outside world. The homosexual has to keep his distance from many people in the outside world. You will force him to keep his distance from you as well.

Does this mean that you should ignore your child's sexual preference? Does it mean you should avoid asking questions about his life and about the meaning homosexuality has for him? Absolutely not. As a reasonable parent, you should be interested in these things, and you'll probably be surprised to find your child is more than willing to discuss them with you. In most cases children desperately want to share their lives with their parents. Many refrain because they are afraid they will be rejected.

During family discussions, be honest. *Under no circumstances* should you lie about how you really feel about your child's homosexuality. Your son or daughter knows that you've been brought up to believe the worst about homosexuality, because he was taught these things as well. He knows that you have mixed feelings about having a homosexual in the family. He also knows that you may be confused about how this came about and what to do about it.

Your son or daughter won't expect you to change your feelings overnight. What your child wants is an honest dialogue with you, an opportunity to talk about the meaning of homosexuality in your lives. If you lie to him he may conclude that he can't trust you. Your dishonesty will have a greater effect upon him than any of the positive statements you make.

It's rare for a gay child to feel rebuffed by his parents because of their negative attitudes, *as long as the parents don't try to make him responsible for their own feelings. Your child is not responsible for your feelings of guilt, or your feelings of disappointment.* You can't make him responsible for how you feel about homosexuality or how you feel about having a child who is homosexual. The same principle applies to your child. If he is old enough to discuss sexual matters and to have sex with whomever he likes, he is old enough to take responsibility for his own feelings, too. Don't let him blame his feelings on you.

What parents and children should do, as in any serious family discussion, is talk honestly about their feelings. It's okay to disagree. It's even okay to get angry at times. But it's not okay to say that your anger is someone else's fault. Talking honestly means being honest with yourself and with others. That's difficult, but remember, you're all on equal ground. It's just as difficult for your child as it is for you.

The Chinese symbol for "crisis" illustrates my viewpoint perfectly. It's a combination of two other symbols meaning "danger" and "opportunity." Every family crisis represents a danger to the stability of the family and a severe challenge to all its members. But the same crisis also represents an opportunity for the family to change and grow as the lives of its members change and grow. Through working with parents and children who come to our counseling center, the Institute for Human Identity in New York City, my colleagues and I have learned about some of the things that parents and children can do to increase their "opportunities" and decrease their fears of the "dangers." Each person in the family has a crucial contribution to make. Whether the crisis will bring more danger or more opportunity depends on all of you.

chapter two

THE VARIETIES OF HOMOSEXUALITY

What is a homosexual? A homosexual is a man or a woman who prefers to develop emotional and sexual relationships with people of the same sex. It is in this area of sexual and emotional relationships that gay people differ from heterosexual people. Many believe, erroneously, that gay people are different in other ways as well. One common fallacy is that one can identify gay people easily, but this just isn't so. Another fallacy is that gay people have no interest in or experience with people of the opposite sex. In fact, most gays develop close relationships with people of the opposite sex, but not for sexual purposes. Some gay people, however, enjoy sexual relationships with both men and women. Such people are often called *bisexual.*

How Many Homosexuals Are There? Social scientists believe that somewhere between five and ten percent of the population of the United States today is gay. That adds up to many millions of men and women. For our purposes it doesn't make any difference how many gay people there are. It would make no difference if there were 100 million or just one million.

For parents, there is only one person of importance, their son or daughter. For parents, the issue is not one of numbers but of lives, and particularly the life of their own child. The quality of his or her life matters more to any parent than the claims of gay liberation organizations about how many gays there are. These groups, and perhaps your son or daughter as well, claim that at least 20 million people in the United States are gay. If your son or daughter is active in one of these groups, you'll find that he or she believes it's very important to make this known. Why do gays care how many of them there are?

Gay people suffer a great deal of discrimination. In the past, gays were burned, hanged, or imprisoned for the crime of loving someone of the same sex. Even today, in what we call our permissive society, a gay person can be fired from a job or arrested for no greater crime than sexual preference. As a gay Vietnam veteran put it, "The army gave me a medal for killing a lot of people, and a dishonorable discharge for loving one person."

In stressing the number of gay people in the United States, the gay organizations wage a war against the discriminatory laws that deny them their civil rights. The claim that their minority group is large gives them greater leverage with our political leaders in the campaign to repeal laws that jail adults for sexual acts in the privacy of their homes, and to pass laws guaranteeing equal rights. But some gay people—a diminishing number, though, again, your child may be among them—need to feel that they are not so different from other people. For them, being different is uncomfortable. By telling you how many gays there are in the country, including those who do not acknowledge their homosexuality, they reduce the feeling that they are different from the majority. Such a son or daughter is likely to stress that many famous people in history were gay. They may also gossip about the sexual lives of current movie stars and prominent Americans as further evidence that homosexuality is rather commonplace.

This information is largely irrelevant to your concerns as a parent. How some movie star acts in public or private is not as important to you as how your son or daughter acts. If your son or daughter were the only homosexual in the world, you would still want him or her to have the best possible life. That's what's important.

Homosexual Stereotypes. What is your picture of a homosexual man? If you were raised in the same way as most of us, you may think of him as a kind of "damaged man." To this way of thinking, a homosexual man is like a woman, he's "effeminate." His interests are unlike those of other men and more akin to womanly pleasures. He's a sissy of the worst sort, afraid of excitement and danger, afraid of hurting his body, and he eschews any kind of contact sport. He may like women, but never in a sexual way. And, if you will allow me some bluntness, the homosexual man of the stereotype prefers to play the role of a woman in bed. According to this image, a homosexual man has given up all his masculine prerogatives to make himself a woman.

The stereotype of the lesbian is comparable to its male counterpart. The heterosexual world perceives the lesbian as a woman who hates her status as a woman and tries to be like a man. We imagine the lesbian as a woman in men's pants, with a man's haircut and a tough-sounding voice. She's the kind of person who's ready to do battle with a man at any time, just to prove that she can overpower him. The stereotypical lesbian wears combat boots and an army sergeant's jacket.

What is interesting about these images is that the gay man and gay woman are both defined as people who are trying to *change their sex.* The gay man is supposed to act like a woman and the gay woman to act like a man.

These simplistic pictures of gay people are used to justify discrimination against them. They are inaccurate representations of the behavior of gay people. They are caricatures of gay people's lives and experiences. But what are gay people actually like?

The first thing for parents and other relatives to recognize is that the overwhelming majority of gay people conform to the usual conceptions of masculinity and femininity. Most gay people could not be identified in any crowd. A homosexual man may be just as competitive in business and sports as the heterosexual. And the lesbian can be just as expressive and warmhearted as her heterosexual sister.

Homosexual men are represented in all the masculine occupations. They are policemen, judges, politicians, athletes and U.S. Army officers. Their speech, mannerisms and goals in life are in conformity with the behavior and goals of the heterosexual population. Many gay people are or have been married, and many of them continue to enjoy rewarding sexual experiences with members of the opposite sex.

Some married gay people live a double life, having a heterosexual relationship within the marriage and homosexual affairs outside it. In the past these affairs were clandestine adventures without the knowledge of the spouse. The homosexual contacts were often transient ones that provided sexual release but not emotional fulfillment. This has changed considerably in recent years, and more married homosexuals are discussing their sexual needs with their spouses. In some cases this adds strength to the relationship. In others, it ends the marriage.

A small but very interesting group of gays do appear to conform to the homosexual stereotype. These are the people, most often gay men, who appear to publicize their homosexuality. This kind of gay man will

give the impression of being as effeminate as the heterosexual world thinks he ought to be. Sometimes outra-
geous in dress and manner, some of these men will dress
in "drag"—women's clothes—and parody the mannerisms of women. They seem to do their best to fit the
stereotype. Why do they do this?

Gay people have always felt rejected by society.
Rejection and discrimination always leave a feeling of
great personal hurt and anger. What does a person do
with the pain and anger built up year after year? There
are two common choices. The first is to suffer deep
depression. When the depression is severe enough, it can
lead to suicide. The second choice is to find a way to
express the anger. But if a gay person is to express anger
he must do so very carefully, to avoid serious punishment. So some gays have developed a technique to
express their anger in symbolic ways. What they do is
make a mockery of the heterosexual demand for masculine conformity. These are the people who seem particularly effeminate, who purposely make themselves appear
frivolous and silly. These are the people who "camp it
up."

Some gays can put on this special hostile face to
the heterosexual world at will: at any gay demonstration
they will start "camping" whenever the police pass, and
then afterward go back to their usual behavior. Others
have behaved this way for so long that it is no longer
under their control. The façade becomes resistant to
change. In time it covers over real feelings and behavior
and takes control of the person. In my experience, the
people who can no longer control this façade are those
who have been hurt and rejected for so many years that
the mask has become a permanent defense. We have little
research yet on this group, but I suspect that they may be
the most sensitive people in the gay world.

Where a direct expression of anger and outrage is

impossible, indirect expression in the form of "flaunting it" works quite well. But it may have disastrous side effects. One cannot live one's life as a parody without losing some control over one's own behavior. In time, the person behind the mask may lose the ability to deal honestly with people, even those he cares for. When that happens, depression may recur. In communities where gay liberation organizations are prominent, gays can express their anger in more direct ways. This is far more desirable for all concerned. In such communities fewer homosexuals turn to the stereotype as a vehicle for expressing anger.

Finally, let us discuss a third type of homosexual. We're accustomed to thinking that each human being acts either like a man or like a woman. But a number of homosexuals (and heterosexuals as well) look beyond the traditional notions of masculinity and femininity. Such people are said to be "androgynous." An androgynous person has the capacity to choose whatever mode of behavior, masculine or feminine, is most appropriate in a particular situation. Androgynous people are usually unconcerned whether their behavior seems masculine or feminine to the outside world. They are concerned only with whether or not the behavior feels natural to them. An androgynous person can be tender and "feminine" when it suits the situation, or stalwart and actively "masculine" when that is more appropriate.

Some people are upset when they see an androgynous man or woman. They look down upon a man who shows interest in the arts or a woman who is more interested in succeeding in business than in raising a family. But the problem here is not the androgynous person, but a biased society that wants a clear distinction between masculine and feminine behavior.

Some people believe that androgyny is the behavior of the future. It will be a long time before we know. In the meantime there is no question that some heterosexuals see an androgynous person as something less than a "true man" or a "true woman." The androgynous male homosexual is more like a woman than some people would like, including some parents. The same is true of the androgynous lesbian, whose masculine traits may be very unsettling to her parents and friends but very functional in her own life.

Gay people make no apology for their androgynous characteristics. Androgyny seems to them to be the most advantageous way to change with an ever-changing world. Whatever the perceptions of the heterosexual community around them, androgynous gay people feel that their ability to adapt themselves to circumstances and situations is a mark of maturity. Such behavior is likely to increase significantly in both homosexual and heterosexual people as time goes on.

To sum up, gay people come from every kind of family, every race, class, religion and nationality. To the best of our knowledge, homosexuals come from all sorts of backgrounds. Gays come from families where one parent is dominant, from families with only one parent, and from families in which both parents divide the power equally. They come from families where there is enormous interpersonal conflict and families where there is unconditional love. Some homosexuals are only children; others have many siblings. Some are star athletes in school and others consider sports a waste of energy. Some gays identify with their fathers and some with their mothers. The one generalization that can be made about gay people is that their personal characteristics and their family backgrounds are as varied as those of heterosexuals.

The
Families

The next several chapters describe the experiences of four families, each of which learned that one of its children was gay. Some reacted to the news in ways that strengthened the family. Others reacted in destructive ways, and both the families and the gay children suffered. I would urge parents to notice what these families did to strengthen or harm themselves. Most of the time we act very judgmentally. On the basis of our own backgrounds, we decide whether another person's behavior is good or bad. If we disagree with what a person does, we blame him for his conduct. In these next chapters I would like you to suspend judgment. Don't blame the people in these families for their attitudes or their behavior. Try to understand how each person felt, and why he acted as he did.

This is one of the most important lessons we can learn in life. When you blame a person for his way of behaving, you set yourself up as his judge. In effect, you're saying that your way of thinking is right and his is wrong. This only leads to arguments. A dialogue between parent and child can become a battle.

A true dialogue requires listening to the other person and trying to understand what he is thinking and feeling. Family battles occur when family members stop listening and start telling the others how they should behave and what they should believe. It's possible to win an argument that way, but you'll never understand your child's homosexuality, and that means you'll never be able to understand your child.

As these family stories show, the "blaming game" is one of the most frequent reactions of parents and children to homosexuality. That's why I'm emphasizing it so much. Too many parents blame their children for what they themselves experience. Too many children blame their parents for their own problems. A family member hurts another family member when he feels hurt himself. He is acting defensively, trying to conceal his injured feelings, by striking back. Parents don't usually intend to hurt their children, nor do children mean to hurt their parents, but sometimes people lose touch with their own feelings, or they're not used to saying how they really feel, or they are too embarrassed to speak directly because it violates an image they have of themselves or the family. But if we can see how we have unintentionally hurt someone else, then we stand an excellent chance of responding constructively to the other person instead of to his anger. When communication is restored, the other person no longer needs to strike out. Perhaps these stories will help you learn how to respond better to your own family.

chapter three

THE PETERSON FAMILY

Amy Peterson was going to visit her daughter in New York. Susan had moved to the city six years ago, and now, at the age of twenty-four, she seemed happy and secure living there. She telephoned her mother fairly often but she rarely visited, and Mrs. Peterson knew why.

Amy Peterson was in her second marriage; the first had ended in divorce thirteen years before. Her first husband, Peter, died in a car accident a year after the divorce. Her daughter and her second husband, Robert, had taken an instant dislike to each other. They never argued or disagreed, but there was no affection either.

As a psychiatric nurse, Amy had often seen family strife, particularly over a divorce, tear a family to pieces. She and her first husband had both been very conscious of this possibility and they had tried to make the separation as easy as possible for Susan, whom they both loved dearly. But Amy had always felt somewhat guilty about the potentially harmful effects of the divorce on Susan, and early in her second marriage she had tried to bring her daughter and her new husband together.

Amy's attempts to encourage friendliness between Susan and her stepfather were abysmal failures. Each of them respected Amy's feelings and remained courteous, but when the two of them were together the atmosphere was unbearable.

At first Amy thought that Susan resented her stepfather as a poor replacement for her real father. It often happens that way. But in time she realized that the problem was more difficult to define.

So Mrs. Peterson decided that it was best to leave things as they were. She saw nothing to gain by trying to force two people to like each other. She knew from experience that her efforts would be stubbornly resisted. This was a wise decision.

When Amy arrived at her daughter's apartment she was surprised to find it cluttered and messy. This was unlike Susan, who had always been a very good housekeeper. But Amy knew better than to comment. Susan was fiercely independent and at the same time sensitive to criticism, especially from her mother. Amy was more concerned about the way her daughter looked. She seemed somewhat depressed but also glad to see her mother, and Amy hoped that Susan would tell her what was wrong without being asked.

As they talked at lunch both of them were as much involved in their fantasies as in the discussion. Susan was considering how much she wanted to tell her mother. Part of her wanted to say things about herself. The other part wanted very much to learn more about her mother. For the moment, learning about her mother came first.

Amy Peterson had done a good job as a mother. Even the divorce, though very upsetting, had not psychologically scarred her daughter. For the past few years, however, Susan had felt distant from her mother. It seemed as if the loving relationship that had always existed between them was over. This was as disturbing to Susan as it was to Amy. Susan wanted to reestablish their good relationship but was uncertain how to go about it.

On three previous occasions Susan had planned to "come out"—to tell her mother that she was a lesbian.

She had rehearsed the scene carefully, writing down objections her mother might have to her lesbianism and the answers she would give. She could answer every objection except one.

Susan was an only child. Every child, a daughter especially, is expected to marry and raise children. When an only child is a daughter, the pressure to marry and raise a family is particularly strong. Susan knew that her mother very much wanted to be a grandmother. Susan knew too that she would never marry, and that this would be a source of continual pain to her mother. No matter how successful Susan might become in other areas of her life, Mrs. Peterson would never be truly happy until she had grandchildren. This was the objection Susan could never answer, and the one that made her feel guilty. She had never been able to tell her mother that she was a lesbian.

Susan's sadness was occasioned by a temporary separation from her lover, Barbara. She had lived with Barbara for a year. They had found an apartment, furnished and decorated it, and they shared a social life.

Neither Susan nor Barbara had come out at work, for they feared discrimination if they did. In their social life, Barbara and Susan avoided the company of heterosexuals. They preferred to socialize with other gay couples with whom they felt comfortable and accepted.

Family holidays presented special problems. Thanksgiving and Christmas dinners were sad occasions for this lesbian couple, as they are for many gay couples. Since they had not yet come out to their families, they could not attend as a couple. As a rule, the lesbian can join the family celebration as long as she comes as a single girl.

Barbara's parents were celebrating their twentieth anniversary, and they wanted her to spend a few extra days at their house. Out of love and respect for them,

Barbara agreed, but she wished that Susan could join the celebration. Barbara felt happy for her parents, and she wanted them to know about her own happiness living with Susan. Sadly, Barbara and Susan agreed that Barbara should go to the celebration alone. Susan would remain at home. That's why Susan was so sad.

On every family holiday the lesbian couple experiences this forced separation. They must either go to separate family gatherings, insist on coming together, or refuse all invitations. They must choose between doing what is best for themselves and respecting the wishes of their families. In most cases the lesbian puts her own need in second place, not wishing to cause the family dissension that would probably result if she insisted on bringing her lover.

Susan and Barbara had yet come to the place in their lives where they were willing to risk telling their parents about their life together. The family relationship each of them had at the moment was considerably better than rejection. So at holiday times Barbara would kiss Susan good-bye and go to the family dinner, pretending throughout that she was single. And when the inevitable remarks were made about her being unmarried when there were so many eligible bachelors around, she bit her lip and smiled. Susan usually stayed at home. She preferred loneliness to a long dinner with her stepfather.

Susan had realized by now exactly why she hated her stepfather. She had never met anyone so adamantly opposed to homosexuality. He was always telling "fag jokes," and once or twice, on family visits to New York, he had tried to pick out the lesbians while walking in Greenwich village. He was an extremely prejudiced man, and Susan had no intention of being in his presence any more than necessary. But to tell her mother why she did not visit them she would have had to tell her everything, and this was one of the reasons she wanted to come out to her mother. It was important to let Amy know that she still loved her.

During the conversation at lunch Susan felt that she could not come out to her mother that day. She felt that Barbara should be there, and she wanted her mother and Barbara to meet.

Susan hoped that by learning more about her mother she could begin to narrow the distance between them. She asked many questions and, to her surprise, Amy answered them all. Susan wanted to know more about her father. What kind of man had he been? What had their early life together been like? Why had they had only one child? What were the problems they had had in their marriage? Mrs. Peterson answered as truthfully as she could. She was nervous about it, but somehow she sensed how important these questions were to Susan, and she too wanted to lessen the distance between them.

Then Susan began asking questions that seriously upset her mother. She wanted to know about Amy's sexual life, about her feelings about sex. Susan wanted to know if Amy enjoyed having sex.

No one had ever asked such questions of Amy Peterson, not even her husbands. But she was even more shocked by the insight displayed by Susan's questions. They had been very crucial ones to Amy throughout her life, and Susan must have sensed that.

Amy was similar to many middle-aged women of her generation. She was brought up in a family that considered sex a dirty affair, and Amy had never been able to rid herself of this burdensome attitude, no matter how she tried. From her own mother Amy had learned that men were driven by sexual needs, and she came to associate sex and aggression, so that sexual acts became aggressive ones in her mind. Sex was something Amy gave to her husband as a favor. It was never a shared experience. She allowed it in order to placate her husbands, and in the hope that it would produce a child, for she had wanted a family of her own.

Mrs. Peterson answered her daughter's questions as honestly as she could, surprising herself with how much information she was revealing. She didn't know where this was leading, but in a few minutes she began to feel pleased with her openness. She sensed that the two of them were sharing something important.

Susan knew that her mother had never talked about sex this way, and she was touched. Much of her own fear diminished. But she wanted to know one last thing. "Mother, are you orgasmic?"

Amy was more frightened by the answer to the question than by the question itself. But she had begun an important conversation with her daughter, and she would not pull back at this point. "Susan, I've never had an orgasm. I've always been so embarrassed about having sex. It was always such a chore. I think that maybe— I'm really very angry at men about sex. Maybe that's why I've never allowed myself to enjoy it. Oh, Susan, that wasn't an easy thing for me to say."

Ironically, as Amy acknowledged how difficult it was for her, she began to feel quite good. She was pleased that she had finally been able to speak about these things. She had carried them around with her for so many years, now that they were said Amy felt immeasurably relieved.

By this time Amy Peterson had regained enough composure to wonder why her daughter was asking these questions at this particular time. Amy knew her daughter, and Susan had always had a way of asking people about themselves when she really wanted to say things about herself. Amy suddenly realized that her daughter was trying to tell her something important.

"Susan, I know you're trying to tell me something, and it must be very important. Won't you tell me what you want to say?"

Susan could not resist this direct question. She had to tell her mother about her lesbianism, no matter what. How could she continue to be dishonest when her mother had been so honest with her?

"You remember Barbara, the woman who lives with me?"

"You mean your roommate?"

"Yes. What did you think about that?"

"I thought she was a nice girl. What are you trying to say?"

"She isn't a roommate. She's the person I love. Mother, I love women."

Mrs. Peterson's immediate reaction was to blame herself for her daughter's lesbianism. She instantly thought of the failure of her first marriage and decided that not having a father around the house explained, at least in part, why Susan had become a lesbian. In seeking the reason for her daughter's homosexuality, she willingly made herself the scapegoat.

Susan saw that her mother wasn't angry or rejecting. She was sad, and Susan guessed why.

"Please don't blame yourself, Mother. I don't know exactly why I'm gay. I'm sure there are causes, just as there are causes of heterosexuality. The important thing is that I'm happy. You always say you worry about me all the time. That I don't have anybody to be close to. But I do. I feel that being a lesbian is what makes me happy, and I'm glad that after years of thinking and learning about it I can finally feel good. Try and believe that I'm pleased with myself. I still need you, and I love you very much. Please believe that—and please try to be happy for me."

Mrs. Peterson had not heard a word her daughter said. The revelation of Susan's secret had been overpowering.

"I don't know how I feel about this, Susan," she

said finally. "I'd like to go home. I need some time to think."

Susan kissed her mother goodbye. She hoped she had done the right thing. She hadn't wanted to hurt her mother, but she had been living for years hiding a very important part of herself. If they hadn't talked about it, their relationship could never have grown.

When Amy got home her husband was still at work. She sat down to think, and all that came to her was "This can't be happening to me." Amy Peterson felt guilty and ashamed. Homosexuals were sick people. They preyed on children. They hated the opposite sex. The list went on endlessly in Mrs. Peterson's mind. She thought of all the stereotypes of homosexuals, never stopping to evaluate how well they fit her daughter. She also thought of the discrimination against homosexuals, and how hard their lives must be, the secrets they must keep, and the guilt they must feel about their sexuality.

Then Mrs. Peterson remembered the large double bed in Susan's apartment, and how excited Susan had been when she talked about buying it. She imagined Susan in the bed, and the other woman, Barbara, lying next to her. She could see the bare shoulders of both women. Then she stopped. She could go no further. But it was this image that made Mrs. Peterson realize that Susan had told her the truth. Amy began to think of her own anger toward men, and her own embarrassment about sex. Very quickly these negative feelings became the embryo of a new idea—that her hostile feelings toward men had caused Susan's homosexuality. She felt intuitively that her daughter's lesbianism was her fault.

At that moment Mrs. Peterson wished Susan had not told her the truth. Had she done it to hurt her? The knowledge that her daughter was a lesbian, combined with the memory of her own marital failures, was more than she could handle. She wanted to confide in someone who could lift the burden of guilt from her shoulders.

She couldn't tell her husband. She knew as well as Susan how much he hated homosexuals. She didn't feel that she could deal with Susan's homosexuality and his prejudice at the same time. But Amy Peterson needed information badly. Nothing had been taught in her nursing school about homosexuality. She had picked up the idea that it was caused by problems in the family, but that was about all. She didn't even know what a lesbian really was.

Amy was particularly worried about what kind of life a homosexual couple could lead. Did they have a family life? Didn't they miss having children? Does one play the man and the other the woman? She thought of silly things, like whether they have friends over for dinner. She wondered what happened when they got old. The thought of Susan old and alone was dreadful.

The next day Mrs. Peterson spent her lunch hour in the hospital library. Throughout the week she spent each lunch time reading whatever articles she could find about homosexuality. To her surprise, she found that the psychiatrists almost never wrote about lesbians. When they wrote about homosexuals, they meant male homosexuals, so she was forced to read about the lives of male homosexuals, assuming that similar things would be true of a woman.

Finally, she came across an article entitled "Homosexuality" in the *American Journal of Nursing,** and it frightened her even more.

> Characteristically, the parents of homosexuals have a poor relationship to each other. The wives are usually hostile, competitive and dominating, and they minimize their husbands. . . .
>   . . . *The major architects of the homosexual pattern are the parents.* [Emphasis added.]

*Irving Beiber, "Homosexuality," *American Journal of Nursing,* 1969, 69, 2637–2641.

Each word was a dagger in Amy's heart. The psychiatrist was saying that she was right to blame herself. Then she read what this psychiatrist thought of homosexual couples:

> Most homosexuals suffer from feelings of loneliness and isolation; none, in my experience, achieve a sense of romantic fulfillment, even when involved in a so-called "love" relationship.

And of these love relationships, he said:

> Such arrangements may include living together, adding such customs as the wearing of wedding rings. These relationships are characterized by initial enthusiasm and intensity of emotional involvement, followed by increasingly frequent periods of conflict. Ultimately, the relationships end in boredom and disillusionment of one kind or another. Few of these liaisons endure for more than a year or two. Sexual fidelity is rare. Even in lasting relationships, the partners seek sexual experiences with others.

That night Amy Peterson had a nightmare.

She was standing in front of a pair of large doors, with a big keyhole in them. A man came over with the keys and opened the doors. He pushed them wide apart. They opened upon a big gymnasium, brightly illuminated with floodlights. In the center of the gym was a row of long tables, and on each table there were four small black caskets. The top of each casket was open, and they all contained dead infants. Around the tables were men and women dressed in black. They were parents mourning for their children, the women beating their breasts. She noticed one woman in particular who was wailing over her dead child Amy walked toward the woman. She stood by the table and saw that the wailing woman was herself, and the dead infant was Susan. Amy awoke, shaking, and realized that she was coming to think of her daughter as dead.

The shock of this realization mobilized her energies, and Mrs. Peterson decided to find out the truth about homosexual relationships, and to find it out at first hand.

At her hospital she had known a nurse who was a lesbian and who, Amy gathered, had been living with her lover for some time. She and Amy had worked on the same floor at the hospital for quite a while. All the other nurses were aware of the woman's sexual preference, though no one talked about it very much. Amy was friendly with her, but she had never inquired about her life as a lesbian.

The nurse and her lover had moved to Florida only a few months before. Amy began to wonder whether her professional relationship with the nurse might be a good enough basis for a visit. Amy decided to seek them out and see for herself what the life of a lesbian couple was like. She asked for a week's vacation and then called the nurse, who was delighted to hear that Amy was coming and suggested that she stay with her. Amy accepted. She also decided that she would not give anyone any indication why she was coming.

That week was a remarkable experience for Mrs. Peterson. Joan, the nurse, and her lover, Margaret, had been living together for the past four years. Although Joan had never married, Margaret had been married for ten years before she divorced. She had three children, two boys of six and fourteen and a thirteen-year-old girl.

Like many people, Amy was under the impression that children raised by a lesbian couple might turn out to be homosexuals themselves. She watched the children carefully. The older boy, Mark, was already stirring sexually, and his interest was clearly in girls. As a matter of fact, it sometimes seemed that that was all he thought about. Like many teenagers in Florida, he spent inordinate amounts of time sunning himself and seemed never to miss a party or any of the weekend Frisbee contests in the park, where all the teenaged boys showed off their young muscles to the girls sitting nearby. Amy would drive Mark to the park and enjoy watching the antics of the teenagers as they went through this playful courting ritual. One Sunday Amy noticed Mark flirtatiously teasing one of the girls, who obviously admired him. Amy could see the obvious sexual interest between them. She suddenly realized how tense she was watching the kids. Amy became aware that she didn't want to see what was happening. The hostile feelings about sex were returning. But this time Amy became fully cognizant of the fact that she was hostile to all forms of sexuality, not just homosexuality. It was an important realization for her.

Margaret's daughter, June, though only thirteen years old, was already interested in boys. The telephone rang constantly, and almost always for June. As for so many girls her age, the telephone was like a lifeline to her girlfriends, and all the gossip of the young teenaged crowd was discussed each night for hours on end. June apparently felt quite possessive about the telephone, all but carving her initials in it. She even asked for a personal telephone of her own. The request was emphatically denied.

The youngest boy, Fitzgerald (called "Fitz"), was only six and still trying to make headway in first grade. He was still a little shaken about the move to Florida, or more exactly, about being taken out of one school and transported to another. Fitz was primarily interested in various bugs that could be found in the back yard. He thought that the larger ones could be trained as pets. The adults were unaware of Fitz's menagerie until screams were heard coming from June's room. Apparently, one of the larger cockroaches had escaped from captivity. Amy soothed the boy's feelings when his collection was banished.

The two older children were aware that their mother was a lesbian and that the woman who lived with them was her lover. Amy wanted to question them about how they felt about this, but she was too polite to. From what she could see, they were unconcerned about their mother's sexual relationship and got along quite well with Joan.

As for Joan and Margaret, they did not seem in any way special. The children were much more interesting to Amy than they were. The women lived a fairly quiet life, taking care of the children, working on the house, and chauffeuring kids from place to place. They were seldom physically affectionate in Amy's presence, though she couldn't possibly know whether this was their way or whether it was because she was there.

The evenings were usually spent quietly at home, but from time to time other gay couples would drop in, pairs of men and of women. There was a bridge game one night a week.

One day Joan asked Amy to go roller-skating, explaining that one of the skating rinks had a special evening for gay people. It wasn't all fun for Amy, who hadn't been on skates for more years than she could remember. Going onto the rink, she stood between the two women, who held her up as they skated around the floor. It took Amy all of ten minutes to get around the rink twice, at which time she decided to watch from the sidelines. Joan and Margaret skated on, enjoying their night out.

In the course of the week Amy saw occasional tensions between the two women as well as the many times when they got on well together. Having been brought up believing that all gay people are excellent at decorating, she was intrigued to find their home furnished rather simply. Their activities as a family seemed no different than those of any other family. There were times, however, when she sensed that financial worries were causing some strain in their relationship.

One evening at supper Amy perceived that Margaret was angry. When the children left the table Amy asked Margaret what was bothering her. Margaret explained that their insurance broker had called that evening to say that he could not get medical insurance for the family. All the companies had turned them down. Margaret was furious because she knew that the insurance companies discriminate against lesbian couples. The only way to get insurance was on individual medical plans, a very costly way of doing things.

Amy was shocked at the obvious discrimination. She asked if this sort of thing happened often. Margaret explained how difficult it could be for lesbian mothers and their children. She was furious that the children were forced to suffer because of the prejudice of insurance executives.

Margaret further explained that banks were reluctant to give loans to a lesbian couple, regardless of their income. It was not always possible to know whether they were being discriminated against because they were women or because they were lesbians, but there was no question that the discrimination existed.

Then, she said, there were times when angry husbands exposed their wives' homosexuality as punishment for leaving them. Husbands sometimes tried by legal means to remove children from their mothers on the grounds of lesbianism. Husbands who did not want the children would sometimes use the lesbianism as grounds for divorce, hoping (and being advised by their attorneys) that the average judge would award lower alimony and child support than would otherwise be the case. A particularly vindictive husband sometimes called the woman's employer to report her lesbianism, and this sometimes resulted in her being fired.

Finally, the neighborhood schools provided problems for the lesbian mother. Insensitive teachers and principals often winked at the tattletale stories that other children told, stories they overheard in their own homes. The children were cruel, but they really did nothing more than mimic the cruelty of the adults around them.

Amy was grateful to Joan and Margaret for speaking about these matters with her. She wanted to understand what the real problems were for lesbians in our society. For the first time, she was finding out, and what she discovered did not fit in with the stereotypes she had learned in childhood.

For Amy, that week took the mystery out of the idea of a lesbian relationship. Joan and Margaret had the same kinds of problems that Amy had had in her own marriages, and they used similar techniques for dealing with them. In spite of all the difficulties of raising three highly active kids on a low income, Amy could see that they loved each other. They seemed a good match, in fact they had been together longer than Amy's first marriage had lasted.

What Amy Peterson saw that week was very different from what she had read in the textbooks. She realized that psychiatrists see gay people only when they are in pain, and that if they used the same standards for all their patients they could say the same things about heterosexuals. She wondered why there weren't books about homosexuals that told a more accurate story. On the plane going home Amy wrote a letter to Susan.

Dear Susan,

We parents are the authorities for so many years that we get used to deciding what's good and bad for our children, even when they're grown up. I know it isn't right but it's hard not to. It's difficult to let your children live their own lives. We fear that if they become too independent we'll lose them. I know I won't lose you, but it's taken a long time to realize that. I've been afraid too. I need love too.

I even wondered if you told me about being a lesbian because you wanted to hurt me. Now I know that isn't true. Then I worried about what my husband would think, the neighbors, and our relatives. I thought about my own feelings, not yours. I thought more about what your lesbianism meant in my life than what it meant in yours. I was being selfish.

You're an adult and you have the right to lead your own life. If you make a mistake, you alone must pay the price. But I want whatever will make you happy, and I don't care what anyone else thinks. In some ways it's not even important what I think about it. It's your life.

I won't lie to you and say that I understand. I don't know how you became a lesbian, and I found out that the experts don't know either. But I'm trying to learn. I also know that I can't wait around trying to understand it. Nothing stays the same in this world, and I have to adjust to the changes. Please bear with me. It will take getting used to.

I don't understand how you feel about other women, but I don't have to understand that. You have to understand it. I think you do. I know we all need someone to love, and if you love a woman, and that's your way of being happy, you're still my daughter.

Amy read the letter over. She thought about some of the expressions she had used and suddenly it occurred to her that she might have been writing the letter to herself as well. Susan had reminded her of how much she had been missing sexually in her own life, and for the first time in many years she was beginning to face this fact. Things were no better in her second marriage. Sex was still a chore.

"If you make a mistake, you alone must pay the price," Amy had written, and she thought of the price she had been paying for so long. Amy decided that when she got home she would talk with her husband about their sexual life and tell him some things about herself that she had hidden. She wasn't going to let her second marriage fail.

As Amy folded the letter and placed it in her pocketbook, she felt very pleased with herself.

chapter four

THE PETERSON FAMILY REVISITED

No term is more universally understood by gay people than "coming out." It is one of the most important decisions a gay person ever makes. There is no analogy to coming out in the heterosexual world, and partly because of this many heterosexuals are unable to understand how crucial it is to their gay children. Coming out is an indication of personal growth and an expression of how a gay person feels about himself and important people in his life. It is not a confession of sexual habits, not a weapon used against the family, not even an act of independence. On the contrary, it is most often an expression of love.

The most important level of coming out is self-awareness. It is the moment when a person begins to accept the idea that he or she is gay. For some people this may be painful, for others it may be only a further self-discovery. It will be especially difficult for the person who has long been aware of homosexual feelings but has tried to suppress or ignore them. Some people fight these feelings with displays of masculinity or femininity, while others identify them as alien intrusions in their lives. Susan, like most women, was not upset when she became aware of her lesbian desires.

The second level is the active desire to have a

homosexual experience, and the willingness to accept responsibility for wanting it. It is not mere sexual experience that indicates a person's coming out. Strangely enough, there are many people who have frequent homosexual experiences but do not consider themselves homosexual. These people have not come out, for they rationalize their behavior in illogical ways.

The third level of coming out brings us to Susan and her mother. It is the revelation of one's homosexuality to other people. It is telling parents, friends, or employers that one is gay. This is often the most difficult level of the process. It is here, in coming out to one's parents, that families may be brought together or driven apart. Sons or daughters may do it all wrong, even though they are well-intentioned; parents may react harmfully, even though they may regret it later. But whatever the reaction of the parents, the act of disclosure stands by itself as a crucial, and sometimes poignant, event in the life of a family. It will certainly change the family in some way. Susan's story shows some of the hazards and the potential benefits of this level of coming out.

Susan was "in the closet," keeping her homosexuality a secret, hiding her sexuality from the world.

Society makes heavy requirements of us all. It expects everyone to be heterosexual and eventually marry. So do our friends and relatives. Susan knew that she was expected to become a wife and a mother, and as long as she was in the closet she had to pretend to meet the expectations of the world. A gay person who has not come out *acts* the heterosexual role, knowing all the time that it is nothing more than an act. The gay person in the closet is forced into a position of dishonesty. It is the lying and deception, the denial of one's natural desire to tell the truth, if not to the world at large then at least to some loved part of it, that makes being in the closet so difficult for most gay people.

Obviously self-protection is one of the most important reasons a gay person stays in the closet. There is discrimination in the world. It's possible to lose a job for no other reason than homosexuality. It's possible for friends to shun a gay person and for some social outlets to close tight. But these problems are relatively easy to deal with. They relate to real dangers in the world, and while some anger must result, it seldom brings long-term emotional harm.

Parents and families are something else again. Deception is most painful where there is love. If this were not so, then a gay child would continue to deceive parents and relatives, caring little about their feelings. The pain results from feeling guilty about pretending that her woman lover was only a roommate. She willfully deceived her mother, and she felt guilty for that. No matter what rationalizations Susan used, she could not absolve herself.

But it is not only the guilt of deception that takes a high psychological toll on people like Susan. There's a higher price to be paid. Susan could never share the good things in her life with her mother. Who better than her mother to tell of the fun and the meaning of furnishing an apartment? Perhaps her mother would shop with her as so many mothers and daughters do? No, the relationship between Susan and her lover might be discovered, and that would create the very crisis Susan was trying to avoid. Who better to tell of the rewards of a love relationship than parents or brothers and sisters? It cannot be told. Who better to tell of the joys of a vacation with one's lover after both of you have saved for a year or two? No, it's better not to show the pictures of the trip—too many questions might be asked. Who better to take to the family dinner at Christmas than the woman Susan loves? But no, it isn't worth the scene. It isn't worth spoiling the dinner for people who do not understand.

Not being able to share the good things is far more damaging to a gay person than the guilt that results from deception.

When someone like Susan wants to stop deceiving her parents, she's right to come out. If she wants to establish a mature relationship with her parents, if she wants to put childhood fears and jealousies behind her, if she wants her parents to become a part of her life, she's right to come out. How her parents will react to the news is a different question entirely. What is important here is that when a child feels caring and love, she has no alternative but to come out.

Susan had been somewhat alienated from her mother for a long time. She wasn't pleased with this distance any more than her mother was. But if Susan had tried to continue a close relationship with Amy, she would have been forced to divulge her homosexuality, and she was not ready to do so. Since coming out is always a voluntary act, the gay person must feel ready to initiate the action. If she's not ready, there's probably nothing a parent can do to relieve the alienation. Susan waited until coming out seemed an integral part of a discussion between mother and daughter.

Fortunately for both of them, Amy Peterson was a bright and intuitive woman. If she had not been, the discussion might have ended on a tragic note. Susan was asking her mother about things that parents and children seldom talk about. But Amy recognized that these questions were important to her daughter, though she didn't know why. If there was anything that touched Susan's feelings of love for her mother, it was Amy's honesty. After that, Susan had no choice but to tell the truth.

Few parents react with indifference when they learn of their child's homosexuality, but the specific reactions can take many forms. Some parents pretend that they weren't told. It's as if they never heard the words, and chances are they will never bring the matter up again. Many parents instantly feel guilty. They believe that anything that happens to their child, especially what they see as bad, is their fault. They assume the blame and ignore the feelings of their child. These parents are not aware that their guilt is a selfish reaction, because it keeps them from hearing what their children are saying, or seeing them as they are, people making an attempt at human contact. Other parents feel anger at their son or daughter's disclosure, and this anger spells trouble for the future. Still others defend themselves against the news by convincing themselves that the child wants to hurt them. As often happens between parents and children, an angry reaction is usually interpreted by the child as an attack, and attacks at this stage are very difficult for anyone to handle. Then there are parents whose first response is to suggest that the gay person see a psychiatrist. Even if this were appropriate, though it seldom is, now is not the time to bring it up. Like parents who respond with guilt, parents who want the child to see a psychiatrist are blinding themselves to the child's real needs. While the parent may see professional treatment as being in the child's best interest, the child is likely to interpret it as a rejection. What Susan wanted to do was talk to her mother, not to a psychiatrist. If Mrs. Peterson had suggested a psychiatrist it would have been equivalent to saying, "I don't want to talk to you about this. Please talk to someone else."

Amy Peterson's response to her daughter's coming out was to block it out. She was so flooded with anxiety that she couldn't cope with the news. As usual when she felt overwhelmed, she buried all her feelings so deep inside her that even she didn't know what they were. Amy, like other people who react this way, became oblivious to her surroundings.

Should Mrs. Peterson have forced herself to talk

with her daughter? Should she have told Susan what was happening to her? People cannot force themselves to do things, especially in a family crisis. People can confront their fears and their difficulties only when they feel ready. How could she possibly talk with her daughter when she didn't know how she herself felt? Just as a gay person can come out only when ready, a parent can deal with his or her own feelings about homosexuality only when ready.

The only thing Mrs. Peterson could do was leave. But what would be the effect of this leaving upon Susan, or any son or daughter? There is no question that many children will experience this as a rejection of them as well as their life-style, but if a parent needs some time to think about what has happened, then he or she should take it. What is most important is what happens in the long run. After Amy got home she began to think about her daughter as a lesbian, and that's when the pain began. At that moment she wished Susan had continued the charade and not disturbed Amy Peterson's equilibrium. Amy didn't want to know about her daughter's homosexuality because she blamed herself for it. She felt that there was something wrong with her, and that she had reproduced her fault in Susan.

When parents are in conflict about themselves, they are likely to blame themselves for anything that happens to their children.

Sometimes they are right, but sometimes the child is at fault, and there are cases, such as homosexuality, in which no one is to blame. But blame is a problem in the dynamics of a family. There are two kinds of "blamers." One kind always claims that the fault lies with someone else, while the blamer plays the role of the victim. The other kind, like Mrs. Peterson, always blames herself and sees the other person as the victim.

Amy Peterson had been blaming herself for a long

time. Since childhood she had had hostile feelings toward men, feelings that had interrupted her development. But these hostile attitudes were only one part of the problem. On another level she felt guilty about having them, and the guilt was a greater source of tension for her than the attitudes themselves. The guilt over her own sexual development set Amy Peterson up as a blamer.

Amy would have blamed herself for anything her daughter did that she didn't like. If Susan had grown up to be a heterosexual woman who divorced her husband, Mrs. Peterson would have blamed herself for the divorce. If Susan had had children and became a child beater, Amy would have convinced herself that she was at fault because she had been a poor model of a mother. The problem was her eagerness to see herself as the cause of all her daughter's problems.

"Self-blamers" do not help their children to accept responsibility for their own behavior. Self-blaming is sometimes used in families to protect the children, as when a self-blaming mother assumes responsibility for the actions of her child, lest anyone think poorly of the child. Self-blame changes mothering into smothering and encourages the child to remain immature. Self-blamers are not necessarily aware of this, nor do they desire it, but it is inevitable. If coming out results in parents' blaming themselves for causing homosexuality, their child is discouraged from talking with them about it ever again. Some parents may actually prefer this state of affairs, but parents who want to understand their gay children will want to learn more about their lives and thoughts.

Amy Peterson's dream interrupted her self-blaming process. That dream mobilized all her strength. Death in a dream is the most powerful symbol we have to represent separation and loss. When Amy awoke she realized that symbolically Susan had died, and the threat of this loss countervailed against her usual self-blaming pattern. This was the moment that saved the relationship between mother and daughter. Instead of thinking about her own feelings, Mrs. Peterson recognized how little she knew about lesbians, and she determined to learn about them and their way of life before judging herself or her daughter.

When the psychiatric information made no sense to her, Amy Peterson made the most important decision possible under the circumstances. She decided to trust nothing but her own judgment.

Her visit to a lesbian couple was the best possible approach for a mother who wanted to learn about the lives of lesbians and the viability of a lesbian relationship. She had the additional experience of visiting a household with children. It is a fact seldom reported by psychiatrists, and mostly unknown to the public, that a very high percentage of lesbians have children. Many lesbians (and some gay men) have been married, and children have been born of these marriages. Since the tradition has been for the mother to take the children when parents separate, lesbians frequently find themselves with the children of their former marriages. It is not uncommon for two lesbians, both parents, to establish a relationship and move into a new home with a houseful of children.

Amy Peterson enjoyed watching the children. She remembered her daughter's childhood and what Susan had been like as she left one childhood stage and went into another. But she also noticed the ways in which children are very different today, how independent and self-reliant they are. And she saw how conspicuously heterosexual Margaret's children were. The lesbian mothers didn't worry about the sexual orientation of their children. The kids seemed to take care of themselves. As for the problems they might experience later in life, Amy felt that Margaret and Joan would be able to handle them.

chapter five

THE CARLTON FAMILY

The Carltons live in a big brick house in a residential section of Chicago. Robert Carlton is a successful businessman, having served for many years as an executive in a large midwestern corporation. His wife, Mary, describes herself as enjoying two occupations, housewife and artist.

One evening as Mary was setting the table for dinner, her four-year-old son, Teddy, came into the dining room. Without a word to his mother, Teddy opened the breakfront that held all the glasses and dishes, took out four small plastic plates and placed them on the dining room table. "I invited them to dinner tonight," said young Teddy.

"Well I hope your friends will behave themselves, Teddy. After all, they are your guests." Mary sometimes wondered what other people would say about a family of three setting six places for dinner. Fortunately it didn't happen every night.

Mary called her husband to the table and the evening ritual began. Young Teddy ushered in his imaginary companions. Many children have one. Teddy had three. The first and most important was Cottage Cheese, a girl a bit older and wiser than Teddy. Cottage Cheese played her part as an external conscience for Teddy, though at times she could be quite a prankster. Naturally she also paid a good deal of attention to Teddy. The two of them were inseparable.

The other companions were boys, Georgie Porgie and Tom Thumb. Since they were younger and not as bright as Teddy and Cottage Cheese, some parental supervision was necessary. Teddy sometimes marveled at how dimwitted they could be. They would do the silliest things, and Teddy had to scold them when they were naughty. This usually happened when things were getting boring around the house. When they were good, Georgie and Tom were allowed to have dinner with Teddy, his parents, and Cottage Cheese. When the family went for a drive the three companions went with them and space had to be provided. Fortunately the Carltons had a station wagon.

Unlike Mr. and Mrs. Carlton, Cottage Cheese did not approve of public displays of affection. She would never kiss Teddy when other people were around, but Teddy saw through her reserve, and he was sure Cottage Cheese liked him. He needed her affection and she was always there to provide it.

Teddy's invention of Cottage Cheese, a girl, was not an indication of problems about his mother. It was only one of the early signs that he admired girls more than boys, and this attitude was to continue throughout his life. To him boys were utterly foreign creatures, while girls impressed him as being smarter and more fun. He made friends with them easily and seemed to understand them better. Boys weren't interested in the things that interested him, and seemed to lack imagination and sensitivity.

These attitudes about boys and their pastimes caused problems for Teddy when he began school. He had no interest in sports and avoided playing ball. Since his father was equally uninterested in athletics, Teddy may have derived this attitude from him. Teddy was more interested in drawing and finger painting than in throwing balls and running around the bases.

Within a short period of time his classmates and teachers managed to change his lack of interest in athletics into a feeling of incompetence. Forced participation in sports only served to make him feel insecure and anxious about performing correctly. He was the last to be picked to play on any team, and his classmates would grimace whenever Teddy was assigned to play on their side. In all of junior high school the only time he got to first base was when he was walked by a poor pitcher.

Teddy was called a "sissy." The other boys treated him as an outcast and once or twice some of the older boys roughed him up. Fighting was particularly difficult for Teddy to handle. He avoided fights whenever possible, and he did whatever he could to make certain that he was not trapped into one. He was afraid of physical violence. Later in life he wondered whether he was a coward, since his feelings about fighting didn't change when he grew up. He looked upon fighting as physical cruelty and didn't understand why he should be cruel to others, or why others were cruel to him. Teddy much preferred to be affectionate and friendly.

It was Teddy's good fortune to be talented in drawing, as well as a good student. In this he was admired by some of the children in his class. He received many compliments from the art teacher. There were also a few boys in his grade who, like Teddy, were uninterested in sports. These nonathletes formed a small band of their own, providing support for each other and ameliorating the teasing of other boys.

Even more than his small band of friends in school, home was the real haven for Teddy. The birth of a brother when Teddy was in kindergarten had provided a replacement for his imaginary companions, and he was already learning how to play with William, the new arrival. Mary Carlton's attitude toward her oldest boy was an excellent antidote to the problems that were arising at school. She was an artist, a sculptor who worked predominantly in clay and plaster. These were wonderful materials for her son to work with. Mary set up a small table in her workshop and bought a few small tools for her son, and each day he would come to his table and make whatever objects suited his fancy. Before supper they would discuss what each of them had done, Teddy frequently wondering why his mother took so long to make something. It certainly didn't take him long. He learned how to make ashtrays out of clay, and he began to produce them at an alarming rate. Within a week every room in the house had at least three of them. Neither Robert nor Mary Carlton smoked.

These afternoons in the workshop were important ones for Teddy. They helped him conquer the feeling of inferiority that he was developing in school. His mother was happy to encourage his artistic sensitivity.

The Carltons were talented in raising their first-born son, and while they made the usual errors that all parents make, they never made any of the more serious ones, such as withdrawing their love in order to frighten the boy into submission. Nor did they ever try to make Teddy feel guilty about his behavior, or pretend that his errors would harm them. Both Mary and Robert liked children, and the arrival of Teddy, and then William, were joyful events in their lives.

For the first few years in school Teddy continued his somewhat distant relationship with boys, except for those who shared his own artistic and academic interests. He was much friendlier with girls. He occupied himself with a variety of activities at home and played with his brother William. The brothers were quite different from one another, and their difference was a source of bewilderment to Robert and Mary. It's not unusual for two brothers to establish very different identities and for these differences to become apparent at an early age. So it was with Teddy and William. William did not share Teddy's artistic interests, and he seldom went into the workshop. He was more interested in playing with friends and competing at sports.

The differences between these two boys did not interfere with the fun they had together. While the usual jealousies and arguments occurred, the Carltons were very good at showing them how to be friends, and the warm relationship between the parents was a model for the boys to follow. Unalike as they were, Teddy and William drew closer as the years went on.

In the sixth grade Teddy found that boys were becoming more attractive. Not more attractive socially, but physically. Although he still liked girls better, he found himself looking at boys' bodies more than he had before. He found the sight pleasing. Occasionally he would go to a swimming class after school at the YMCA. This provided Teddy with the opportunity to experience new physical sensations. He loved watching the other boys running naked in the shower room, and the occasional wrestling matches in which they rubbed their bodies against each other. Both the visual stimulation and his physical response were a source of enormous pleasure. Teddy had never had this kind of interest in girls. Boys were something else. His attendance at swimming class improved.

By the time he entered junior high most of the boys were interested in sex. *Playboy* magazine was popular with the boys in Teddy's school. Little groups would huddle in the schoolyard peeking at the center-fold. Teddy waited patiently until the other boys had finished looking at what interested them. Then he would take the magazine to a quiet place and look at the underwear ads for men.

By the time he was fourteen Teddy knew that he was gay. His sexual fantasies were all of boys. When he masturbated he thought of a boy in his class at school, whom he imagined nude at the swimming pool or on the athletic field.

Teddy felt ambivalent about his homosexual fantasy life. On the one hand he was used to the feeling of being different. He had been different all his life, and the homosexual fantasies were only another instance of his divergence from social norms. The pleasure of masturbation further encouraged him in the direction of homosexuality. Since his parents never taught him to feel guilty about himself or his body, he thought of his homosexuality as a natural consequence of growing up.

But there were other feelings that began to intrude. He was certain that his sexual enchantment with some of his school friends would never be realized. He was old enough to know that homosexuality was condemned by all those around him. And he was very conscious of the teasing words he heard in school, words boys use so frequently to taunt each other, like "queer" and "fag." Being different than other boys had become too much of a burden for Teddy.

By the time Teddy entered high school he was feeling lonely and isolated from his peers. At this age, when boys try so hard to be part of their peer group, Teddy wished to be more fully accepted and he yearned to participate more actively in the social life at school. Teddy felt jealous of his younger brother, who appeared far better integrated socially than he. Teddy wanted to be popular. To achieve these goals, he designed what he called "The Self-Betterment Program," a rather extraordinary attempt to broaden his social life. While continuing his strong academic performance, Teddy added a personal program of athletics and social engineering. He continued to participate in swimming (though he had ambivalent feelings about his sexual interest), and he went out for soccer practice every day after school. He made friends with the members of the soccer team, and they became frequent visitors at the Carlton house. In this way he hoped to become more socially acceptable.

The "social betterment" part of the program posed more difficult technical problems. Teddy had to show sexual interest in girls at school and be able to perform sexually.

Teddy's plan was quite ingenious. Teddy invented a technique to condition his sexuality toward women. He bought a number of *Playboy* magazines and kept them in his room. Each night he would undress and look at the pictures in *Playboy*. While he looked at them he played with his penis until he had an erection. Then, applying a lubricant, he massaged it, still looking at the pictures of the nude women. As he masturbated, he kept imagining that he was having sex with the woman he was looking at. If his excitement lessened, he would think of a boy he was interested in, then return to the woman. He resolved to ejaculate only to the fantasy of the naked woman. It didn't work.

After a while Teddy became so frustrated that he had to admit that this part of the program was not succeeding. After that, he masturbated with the image of whole teams of athletic stars dancing in his room. But he didn't give up on the rest of his program. Soon afterward he had his first heterosexual experience, with a student at his school. He had no difficulty maintaining an erection, or in reaching orgasm. To Teddy's inexperienced eyes, the girl appeared to enjoy it. But Teddy found the experience uninspiring. The girl was pleasant enough, and the orgasm was enjoyable, but the experience was not filled with excitement. As a matter of fact Teddy's masturbation fantasies were more exciting than the heterosexual experience. As he went home that evening, Teddy wished he could have a sexual experience with a man. He wondered how he would feel having sex with a man.

A couple of weeks later Teddy and a female cousin (to whom he had confided his homosexuality) went to see a film. As they stood in line outside the theater, Teddy saw an attractive man in his early twenties just a few feet ahead of them. He seemed to be alone. Teddy was attracted to this man, and when he turned around and smiled, bells started ringing. The three of them began talking, and by the time the line moved into the theater they felt like old friends.

As they sat inside watching the film, Teddy wondered what to do next. This was all new to him.

Teddy knew the man was gay. He just did. He was equally certain the man knew the same of him The sexual vibes between them were strong. This was the opportunity he had waited for for so long. He leaned over to his cousin and asked what he should do. She suggested that after the movie Teddy propose that the three of them go out for coffee. She'd decline with an appropriate excuse, and Teddy and his new friend could go off by themselves.

As they left the theater Teddy suggested they all go out for a drink. His cousin quickly declined, allowing Teddy and the young man to go off together.

Late that night Teddy decided to walk home instead of taking the bus. He needed time to think about what had happened that evening. It was incredible. His body had been on fire the whole time he spent with Peter. Those few hours of making love with a man had confirmed everything that Teddy believed about himself. He also knew that, unlike the experience he had had with a woman only a short time before this, could not be equaled by masturbation. Actually, holding another man in his arms, and being held in his, was far more satisfying in reality than in fantasy.

As Teddy was walking down the street he met a couple of friends from school. He chatted with them amiably for a few minutes and then continued home. He wondered where his friends had been that night, and whether they had had sex and with whom. He wondered whether they could tell that he had. Teddy's sensitive nose could smell the odor of sex about him, and he wondered if the others could smell it too. The odors of the body, particularly during sex, were like aphrodisiacs, and his appreciation of them heightened his sexual response. Teddy also wondered whether his friends could tell that his odors were homosexual, not heterosexual. That would be all right too. He felt good about being gay. It was partly the feeling of being different that pleased him, but it went beyond that. That night Teddy felt he was his own person, a special kind of guy, someone who had discovered that his fantasies and desires could be realized. That night Teddy knew that he was truly gay, and that he liked it that way.

Teddy hadn't just come out that night. He had galloped out! He went to the city every weekend, and it didn't take long to find out where gay people looked for sex. Like a child with a new toy, Teddy plunged into the world of sex enthusiastically. In the course of the next few months he had many sexual experiences. Almost all of this sex was of the "quickie" variety, but after this playful marathon of sexual prowess, Teddy started to look for men who could provide for his emotional as well as sexual needs.

When Teddy embarked on this search, he thought of his parents as the model relationship. It was then that he thought of coming out to them. He wanted to tell his parents about his homosexuality because he wanted to share this part of his life with them. Although Teddy had been happy the past few months, he was unable to discuss this happiness with the people he loved most of all, his parents and brother. Whenever the family gathered, Teddy would feel restrained, unable to say things he knew they would want to hear.

He was uncertain how his parents would react. He knew that he wouldn't be punished. That was not the Carlton style. But by now he had already heard many stories from gay friends in Chicago who had come out to their parents, only to see them brutalize themselves with guilt and shame. He wondered if his parents could accept his homosexuality as well as he did. After all, they belonged to a different generation and might not be able to understand how things were now.

At that point Teddy realized that he was treating his parents as if they were children. He was trying to protect them, and that attitude showed no confidence in their maturity. Since they had never acted selfishly toward him, it was unfair to treat them in this way. Just as Teddy had the right to learn through experience what kind of sexual life he wanted to lead, so his parents had the right to know of his decision. As long as his discussion with them was motivated by the desire to share, any problems they experienced would not be his fault. He decided to tell them about his sexual experiences and his plans for the future.

One night after dinner he told his parents that he had something to discuss with them. It was just Teddy's luck that commotion reigned that evening. The dishwasher broke down, and they had to do the dishes by hand. William was convinced that he was going to flunk his exams the next day, and was demanding sympathy for his plight. Robert Carlton was repainting the den. It was only hours later that Teddy found the opportunity to come out to his parents. Mr. and Mrs. Carlton were starting to bed when he said, "Wait a minute, I want to talk to you." There was a note in Teddy's voice that instantly told Mary Carlton that this was important. Her first guess was that he was having a problem with one of his girl friends. He still had many. Neither of his parents anticipated the news they were about to hear.

They went up into the Carltons' bedroom and Teddy told them everything he had felt and experienced from the time he first got excited in the pool shower room to his first homosexual experience in the city. He told them of his cruising for quickie sex. He wasn't certain how much to say about the things he actually did in bed. For the moment he decided to leave out the specifics.

Mr. Carlton's first reaction was, "Are you sure?" He asked Teddy whether it was only a passing interest. Teddy unambiguously said that this was no phase. Mrs. Carlton, as surprised as her husband, asked if Teddy would like the opportunity to speak to a psychiatrist. Teddy responded by saying that a psychiatrist couldn't help him because he felt very happy with his life. He had never felt happier.

Both parents understood Teddy's reasons for coming out to them that night, and they were sure that he had given them an accurate picture of his emotional and sexual life. They never again questioned whether he was gay or suggested that it was a passing phase.

As so often happens, Mary Carlton's strongest reaction was guilt. She thought she must have done something wrong for Teddy to have become a homosexual. Her religious upbringing, with its condemnation of homosexual behavior, was one of the first things she thought of. The guilt fostered by the church and the little bit she had heard about homosexuality made her feel at fault. She remembered the time she had tried to push Teddy into joining the Little League. How he hated it. Perhaps she shouldn't have pushed him that way. She also wondered whether she had been too bossy.

Robert Carlton saw his wife's distress immediately and responded to it. He told her that he believed homosexuals were born, not made; that he had never accepted the notion that family troubles made a child a homosexual. Somehow a person was born either homosexual or heterosexual, and attempts to fight this inborn disposition were doomed to failure. He added that he considered a person's basic character more important than his sexual orientation. The parents are responsible for building character and nothing more. This was very helpful to Mrs. Carlton. Feeling somewhat relieved, she started to talk to Teddy, who had listened quietly to the exchange between his parents. She wanted to know whether he felt resentful about anything she had done in the past. She really wanted to know how he felt about her right now. Teddy sensed what she wanted and said, "I love you just as much now as I ever have." The reassurance from both Teddy and his father assuaged what guilt there had been.

Robert Carlton began to talk about his college days, when one of his friends had been homosexual. It was then that he had discovered how difficult life could be for homosexuals. Mr. Carlton was not homosexually inclined himself, but for some reason he never felt threatened by homosexuals. He'd had a good relationship with this friend in college, but others in the dormitory were not so understanding. His friend was alternately teased and shunned, and sometimes beaten up. He was discriminated against in the most flagrant and violent ways, and finally driven out of the school. Robert Carlton never forgot how ugly people can be, how prejudiced toward another person who has never harmed them.

"Look," he went on, "you know this may be very difficult for you. Not because of your own feelings but because of how some other people can act. People may dislike you because you're gay. They may never give you a chance to show what kind of person you are. They may make fun of you or try to hurt you. And you probably won't be able to do anything about it. Are you prepared for that?"

"I've already witnessed that discrimination, Dad, I

know about it. I think I know how to pick my friends, and I can't stop living my life because other people don't like me."

There was nothing more to say that night. Teddy kissed both his parents and returned to his room. Robert and Mary talked a bit more, and went to sleep knowing that other issues would be raised later.

Teddy was glad that during the next week his parents weren't trying to discuss homosexuality with him all the time. It wasn't that he was unwilling. He just didn't want his sexual orientation to become the focus of his family life. Some children might have reacted differently. They might have felt that their parents were trying to avoid the issue, to deny its importance in their lives. But Teddy knew this wasn't the case. They would talk about it when necessary.

It became necessary toward the end of the week. The Carltons wondered whether William should be told about his brother's homosexuality. They discussed the issue with Teddy. They were all worried William might find out through gossip in the community, and that seemed intolerable. Teddy decided it was his responsibility to come out to his brother.

William was five years younger than Teddy. He was the athlete of the family and a social leader in his school, and peer pressure would exert a great effect on him. He was very sensitive to other people's attitudes, and he was more conforming than anyone else in the family. If anyone was vulnerable to teasing about having a "queer" for a brother, it was William.

Teddy was right about William. When he was told he gave no outward reaction, but inside he was crying. He could already feel the ostracism by his friends in school. For the next week he said little to Teddy, asked no questions, and moped around the house. Teddy knew enough not to invade William's privacy, but he wished that William would do or say something so they could talk more about it.

He finally did. He came into Teddy's room and said how difficult it was for him to have learned that Teddy was gay. He looked up to Teddy so much that it hurt him to think that his older brother was that different from everybody else. But the feeling of family solidarity was stronger than the problems he anticipated at school. His love for his brother was more important than any comments that might be made. He would just have to deal with things as best he could. Then, as a gesture of loyalty, he asked Teddy for a gay liberation button. He wanted to wear it in school to show his friends that he was on his brother's side.

Tears came to Teddy's eyes as he embraced William and thanked him. It made him feel wonderful, Teddy said, to know that his brother was willing to make that kind of sacrifice. But he suggested that maybe it was a little premature. No need to rush things.

After graduation from high school, Teddy entered the University of Chicago to major in fine arts. Teddy wanted the freedom to live with other college students rather than at home, and so he and a few friends rented a small apartment not far from the college campus. During his freshman year Teddy joined the college gay liberation group and widened his knowledge and experience of gay life-styles and relationships.

One day Teddy came home for dinner and announced that he was going steady with another boy at the university who was also an artist. Teddy wanted to invite his lover to the family Thanksgiving dinner. The Carltons felt that they could not refuse their son's request. They were not really certain how they felt about Teddy's love relationship with another man. Indeed, they didn't know what it meant for two men to be in love with one another. It was outside their own experience. But this was reason enough for them to invite Teddy's lover, Michael. They wanted to know what it meant to Teddy to have a lover, and they thought this an excellent way to find out.

Michael's homosexuality had not been well received by his own family, and he was wary of meeting Teddy's. He felt awkward about going to a strange house and meeting the parents of the man he loved. He didn't see how the meeting could help his relationship with Teddy. But, like the Carltons, he felt he could not refuse. Teddy had successfully disarmed all parties concerned. With his small college allowance he bought the best bottle of wine he could afford. He took Michael by the hand and said, "Everything will work out wonderfully."

As they walked through the front door of the Carlton home, Teddy and Michael were holding hands. More accurately, Michael was squeezing Teddy's hand, fearful of the encounter and very worried that the Carltons wouldn't like him and that he would create problems between Teddy and his parents. Michael had dressed well for the occasion, with a white shirt, tie and carefully pressed slacks and sport jacket. He had to look incongruous next to Teddy, who, being more relaxed about the situation, wore a flannel shirt, jeans and sneakers.

The first to greet them was William, in dress a mirror image of Michael, since he too was worried that he would make a poor impression on Michael and thereby hurt his brother's feelings. William graciously invited the guests into the living room (as if his brother didn't know where it was) and called his parents.

The first hour was very long. The conversation consisted of demographical and statistical questions and comments. Mary Carlton tried to make Michael feel more comfortable by asking him about his interest in art and the kind of work he did. Michael answered each question carefully and succinctly and then stopped, waiting for the next question. Mary realized that she had placed herself in the position of an interrogator, when she had only wanted to put the boy at ease. The conversation was stilted because everyone was being careful not to say anything that would hurt someone else. No one felt relaxed. Mary decided to take the first plunge.

"Oh! I feel so bad. Michael, you look so nervous and tense. We don't want you to feel that way. We want you to have a good time with us tonight. Teddy says that he loves you, and he's never said that about anyone except us, so we know that you must be very special to him. We're so afraid that we will do something wrong and that Teddy will feel hurt. How can we make you feel at home?"

It was not the words spoken by Mary Carlton that disarmed Michael, it was her tone. Michael could hear how distressed she was, and he felt more comfortable knowing that she was as uncomfortable as he.

"Can I take off my tie?" There was a whispered quality to the way Michael said this, a quality that indicated he was making fun of his own nervousness. It was a perfect time for humor, and everyone laughed. Ties came off and everyone began to relax. Mrs. Carlton then brought the family into the dining room for the Thanksgiving meal.

The conversation during the meal flowed more freely. Teddy directed much of the discussion to the decorating of the apartment that he and Michael shared. Both Mr. and Mrs. Carlton joined in with ideas of their own, but part of the time they were lost in their own thoughts. They wondered how they felt about this young man who had become their son's lover, and they wondered if they would have reacted differently if he had brought home a woman. But they realized that both the boys were still young, and they were well aware that this love relationship might or might not last. Only time would tell.

Robert and Mary Carlton could not help noticing the number of times Teddy and Michael touched each other during the meal. They also were alert to the special way in which these two boys looked at each other. There was no question that they cared for one another and that this caring was important to both of them.

After the meal Michael asked to see the workshop where Teddy had spent so many happy hours in his childhood. Teddy had spoken of it so often. William volunteered to take Michael there, probably the only time in his life that he would have made such an offer. Teddy remained behind with his parents.

"I hope you like Michael."

Mary Carlton responded by saying, "I don't know yet. I don't know yet. It's too soon for me to know exactly how I feel. I know there isn't anything about him that I don't like. But I have to get used to seeing him as your lover, not your friend."

Robert Carlton's reaction was different. "I want you to find someone to love. I think I would be happier if you loved a woman, but I know that won't happen. If you're going to love a man, I want it to be someone who can return your love, and only you can know that. So in a way it doesn't make any difference what I think. The most important thing is for you to know if you want to share your life with Michael or anyone else. Your mother and I love you—now you have to choose the man who will love you, and make your lives together."

As Michael walked back into the dining room he could see Teddy kissing his mother and father. Michael hesitated for a moment, wondering whether he should intrude. Robert Carlton called him into the room. Teddy took Michael by the hand and said, "I think you're going to be part of my family as well as my lover."

chapter six

THE CARLTON FAMILY REVISITED

Sugar and spice and everything nice, that's what little girls are made of. Snips and snails and puppy-dog tails, that's what little boys are made of.

We've always expected our children to act very differently, depending upon whether the child is a boy or a girl, and children are taught this from the time they are born. Mothers expect their daughters to adopt feminine ways and interest themselves in family life. Fathers expect their sons to excel in sports and other competitive activities. When psychologists talk about sex roles they mean teaching a child how a boy acts, or how a girl acts, and then getting the child to judge himself or herself by the sex-role standard taught in the home.

The trouble with sex roles is that not all children act the way they're supposed to. Teddy Carlton would have laughed at the rhyme. It had no meaning in his life. The fact is that most children are quite different than we believed in the past. Little boys sometimes want to play with girls and with dolls, and more than one girl has challenged a boy to a footrace—and won. There are even children who seem alternately to adopt both masculine and feminine behaviors. Though parents are sometimes perplexed by this, to children it seems so natural that they are confused by the fuss that parents can kick up.

Teddy Carlton is an example of a boy who displays both masculine and feminine behavior. We're recognizing more and more boys and girls like this. Whereas adults may have punished these children in the past and prevented them from developing according to their natural inclinations, today parents are allowing their children to grow in their own ways.

Throughout his childhood Teddy combined sensitivity and independence in a way that cannot be described as typically masculine or feminine. Teddy's imaginary companions are a clear example. It was no accident that his favorite was Cottage Cheese, a girl. Nor was it accidental that there were boy companions as well. At that age Teddy was developing his own personality and expressing his own perception of the differences between boys and girls. In a sense Teddy was contributing to his own socialization process. We used to think that parents and other adults were the only source of a child's understanding of how to behave. We're now finding out that some children make up their own rules, quite apart from what the adults in his life contribute. Children have probably always done this, but we adults are just learning about it now.

Teddy's early preference for girls began with Cottage Cheese but soon embraced girls in general. Does this mean that he identified only with girls? Does it mean that he wanted to be a girl? Was this something that his parents should have worried about? The answer to all these questions is no. Teddy didn't want to be a girl. He much preferred to be a boy, but he shared some attitudes with girls. Girls in general were more interested in the studies he liked, and they tended to be less violent than boys. Teddy could always feel more comfortable with them as friends because of these characteristics. What could be more natural than to find the boy associating with the children to whom he felt most closely attuned? Such a child is delicately tuned in to his own personal needs, and he seeks to satisfy those needs whether adults like them or not.

Some parents, and particularly fathers, are upset by children like Teddy. They feel very uncomfortable if their son is "playing house" with the girls; he should be throwing balls with the boys. Such parents often insist on forcing the child to act "like a boy."

Parental pressure could have been a very serious problem for Teddy Carlton. It is usually parents' reactions to this type of child that set the tone for the child's emotional development. The Carltons, for instance, could have discouraged Teddy from spending time with Cottage Cheese, or even discouraged the boy from having any imaginary companions. They could also have insisted on his being more competitive than he wished. They could have discouraged Teddy's association with girls, teaching him, as many parents do, that playing with girls would mean he was a sissy.

Many young boys are called sissies at one time or another, but if this happens at home the psychological damage can be severe. When parents call their child a sissy they are telling him that he is not loved. Most often they are worried about his learning the proper male behavior so that he will grow up to be effective in the world. Parents who do this are well-meaning people who want to teach their children, not hurt them. But regardless of the motivation, their attitude is experienced by the child as rejection. In extreme cases the child becomes fearful of the parents and actively avoids them.

Mr. and Mrs. Carlton were not upset about Teddy's behavior. They accepted his imaginary companions, though there must have been some very trying moments. They were not upset about his friendships with girls at an age when most boys disliked them. Mr.

Carlton was not the kind of man who demanded that his son engage in typically masculine pursuits. He allowed the boy to develop in his own way.

Robert Carlton is the real hero of this story. He is a most unusual man, and Teddy's good adjustment throughout his life can be attributed in part to how well Robert Carlton reacted to him. Mr. Carlton was never disturbed by his son's departures from stereotypical male behavior. His goal for his son was the development of a capacity for independent judgment and action.

There aren't many fathers in our society who would have been as calm as Mr. Carlton was at the possibility that his son might reject many conventional male values. Part of the answer probably lies in the fact that Mr. Carlton as a child shared some of Teddy's traits.

Unfortunately Teddy's schoolmates and teachers took a different attitude. That's when the problems began. Children like Teddy are noticeably different from other children. This is especially true of young boys because their behavior stands out more than the behavior of androgynous girls. Young girls have always been allowed to be "tomboys," but no acceptable analogy exists for boys.

Until Teddy entered elementary school, he had no worries. But the constant cries of "sissy" and the taunts of the other boys changed an indifference to sports into a feeling of inferiority. For the first time in his life he was afraid of physical injury. His excellent academic performance could do nothing to ameliorate the teasing.

As a culture we hold some values that are both strange and inconsistent. Our attitude toward young boys is one of them. Here was a child with a personal set of values that would have been admired if he had been a man. But in a boy these values were condemned.

By what strange form of logic do some of us say that a grown man who shows sensitivity and warmth is a

man of character, but a boy who does the same is a sissy?
Like other children who are different, Teddy shied away
from his age-mates because they demanded conformity
to standards that he could not accept.

Children like Teddy are not necessarily antiathle-
tic. They seem so because athletics in our schools are
basically team-oriented, competitive and combative. The
androgynous boy is not likely to be interested in beating
another person at a game. He is frequently perplexed at
being forced to play a team sport when he prefers to play
alone. The joy some schoolboys take in their physical
prowess is a complete mystery to a boy like Teddy. There
was no way that he could understand how unrestricted
aggression between two boys on a playing field could be
called sport. If interested in athletics at all, androgynous
children are likely to prefer tennis, gymnastics, swimming, or track.

The general rule to keep in mind is that children
who do not conform to the social norms in school are
likely to be perceived as "antisocial" by some teachers
and by many of the children. The greater the emphasis on
competitiveness in the particular range, the more the
androgynous child will feel oppressed. By and large,
most children are conformists in school, and noncompet-
itive children, as well as highly creative ones, may end
up with few, if any, friends. Even worse, they find that
there are no children or adults in the classroom who can
validate their lives—that is, let them know that their
pursuit of their own interests is good and that they
should continue to grow in their own way. Validation
means telling the child that it's okay to be different from
other children. In a classroom it means that differences
between children are encouraged and not punished.

A child's home should always be a place of safety.
But the home has an extra task when the school fails to
respect the child's differentness. If an androgynous child

is treated as badly at home as he is in school, the effects can be disastrous. Rejection by playmates, teachers and parents is usually too much to handle, and the inevitable result is a lonely and chronically depressed child. Teddy was accepted and loved in his home. It was the one place where no one demanded that he try to be someone else's idea of a boy. Since the Carltons felt so strongly about teaching their children independence, they encouraged Teddy to be as different as he wished to be. They did not discourage conformity, but they didn't insist on it.

The conflict that Teddy experienced between his home and his school was reflected in his conflict about his homosexuality. Teddy was uncomfortable about his gayness only insofar as he began to feel like a social outcast in school. It was not homosexuality *per se* that was a problem, it was the social perception of homosexuality.

There are some general characteristics common to families of youngsters who are guilt-ridden about their homosexuality. However, we should keep in mind that every family is unique, and every person within a family is different from the others. Generalizations must be tempered by consideration of the circumstances in each particular family.

One of the characteristics of children who are troubled by their homosexuality is their adherence to social norms. In contrast to a child like Teddy Carlton, these children submit to peer group pressures. They are children who learn "the rules" early in life, and they believe in them. Generally they are interested in the conventional occupations of their sex, they believe in marriage, and most important, they believe that the behavior of men and women should be very different. The more they see themselves as diverging from the stereotype of their sex, the lower they fall in their own eyes

Peer pressures on this sort of person are just as strong in adulthood, and such people are likely to keep their homosexual preference very secret. Some of them will never divulge their homosexual desires to family, spouse, or friends. They pay a very heavy price for the burden of self-hatred they carry. The secrecy of their lives compounds their problems, and they spend enormous energy maintaining a false front.

By and large, guilt most strongly characterizes the psychological makeup of these gays. We don't have very much research yet about their families, but we might surmise that guilt is used excessively. Such people are driven by the idea that they are guilty of the most horrible crimes. Some of them may never have had a homosexual experience.

Finally I should mention that some children feel guilty about sex regardless of the sexual object. Some parents are very poor models for learning about sexual attitudes. Children from these families are likely to experience all sexuality in an ambivalent way. Masturbation is usually the act that initiates their guilt. Teaching a child to feel guilty about his or her sexual desires and sexual organs will lead to guilt about all sexual behavior, whether it conforms to local social standards or not.

The Carltons were a good model of healthy adult sexuality. Their reaction to their son's homosexuality showed this clearly. They had never suspected that Teddy was gay. His attitudes toward women had always been good, and they had assumed that his sexual desires were heterosexual. While they had always recognized the marked differences between Teddy and his younger brother, there was no reason for them to think that Teddy's sexual preference would incline toward men. They were well aware of Teddy's frequent trips into Chicago and how particularly pleasant he was around the house afterward. They assumed that he was sexually active in the city, but this was something they would not have asked about.

The Carltons felt very strongly that each person has a right to privacy, and this included the children. Unlike some parents, they believed that children should not be pressured into divulging their secrets. The Carltons trusted Teddy's judgment and self-reliance. They knew that their son felt free to discuss anything he wanted to with them, and this knowledge was sufficient for them.

Mr. and Mrs. Carlton allowed Teddy to tell them as much about his homosexuality as he wanted to in their first discussion, and that was a great deal. For some parents it would have been too much. But the Carltons listened. It's difficult enough for a child to discuss his homosexuality with his parents; it becomes impossible if the parents interrupt him with questions and comments. We cannot know if the Carltons listened out of wisdom or because they were shocked, but their patience was very important. Most children who come out to their parents are afraid the parents won't understand, and constant questioning will sometimes give them the feeling that they have done it all wrong and only caused grief and confusion.

When Teddy finished his story his father said, "Are you sure?" Mr. Carlton's reaction was directed toward his son, not himself. Even when he discussed the discrimination against homosexuals, he was motivated by the desire to give information to his son, not the desire to change him. Some parents might have used social prejudice as an argument against homosexuality, but Teddy knew this was not his father's intention.

Mrs. Carlton's first response was a feeling of guilt, as if she were to blame for her son's sexual preference. She suggested a psychiatrist. But when Teddy rejected the idea, she accepted his decision. Just as important was her need to know how Teddy felt about her. Since she honestly feared that he might be resentful toward her, it was crucial to ask him, and she chose the right moment. That question is not easy to ask when a parent feels she may be responsible for a child's troubles, but if she hadn't asked she would never have been able to rid herself of the idea that she had done something terribly wrong. Mrs. Carlton's distress was noticed by both her son and her husband, and they came to her rescue.

What is most constructive about this coming-out discussion is its openness. The worries and concerns of each person were expressed that night, and there was no attempt to hide feelings. We can see how solidly this family worked together to keep the love and security of the family intact.

The Carltons, like all parents with a gay child, had to face the question of whether to tell other family members. The Carltons didn't make hasty decisions, and Teddy and his parents discussed the question together. Teddy rightfully felt that he should be responsible for telling his brother, who had a right to be told.

Parents should not assume the child's responsibility for telling siblings about his or her homosexuality. If the parents do, they implicitly suggest that there is something wrong about it. No one can present the issues as well as the gay child, and even if s/he balks at the idea, it should be the child's responsibility. In circumstances where a gay person is upset about being homosexual, parents should be sensitive to timing, and if explaining at once is too painful, the issue should not be pressed.

When siblings find out that a brother or sister is gay they are as diverse in their reactions as parents are. Prudent parents will watch those reactions carefully. At one time we could have been sure that siblings would be very unhappy with the news of a brother or sister's homosexuality, especially an older brother. But times have changed, and so have the attitudes of today's youngsters. They have been brought up in an atmosphere where sexual matters are discussed far more freely than before.

Children now are likely to react in very positive ways. They will probably be supportive to the gay child, and to their parents. As parents, you should listen to the heterosexual son or daughter. Their reactions can be very helpful to you.

Not all children react positively. Some are upset by the news. It's important for both the parents and the gay person to understand why. There can be many reasons: For one, some siblings fear that homosexuality may be genetic or contagious. (No one need have taught this to them; children can dream up their own theories without help from adults.) If this is the case, then the parents and the gay sibling should cooperate to reassure the child that s/he will grow up in his or her own natural way.

Some siblings are afraid their gay brother or sister has become different in some way that will change their relationship. Here the gay child carries the full burden of demonstrating that this is not so.

In the Carlton family it was William who was shaken by the news of Teddy's homosexuality. As Teddy had predicted, William was highly sensitive about his social standing in his school and community. Teddy was again correct in wanting to be the one to tell William, even though it could have meant a painful scene. While parents can be useful in smoothing over some of the difficulties, they cannot be as helpful as the child who is gay. Brothers and sisters develop a way of talking to one another, and their face-to-face discussions cannot be replaced by even the most well-meaning parents. Parents can and should assist when either of the children asks it. They can help their children to talk to one another about the situation, and insist that each of the children has a right to his own feelings. If parents find that one of their children is deeply disturbed at finding out that a brother or sister is gay, they should indicate to the child that they understand these feelings and welcome talking about them. Most of all, parents should recognize that, just as they know their children and their moods, so the children know the attitudes and moods of their parents. I strongly suggest that parents not lie to their other children, even if their attitudes about homosexuality are negative. Children know when their parents are lying to them. And if the parents lie to the child, how can the child be truthful with the parents?

Remember that any son or daughter who is upset is in need of support and love. Whatever the disturbance, the child needs to know that it's okay to feel that way, and to be reassured that the gay brother or sister hasn't suddenly become an alien. Parents should recognize that the responsibility for providing this support must be shouldered by them as well as the gay child.

Meeting your son or daughter's lover is no more of a problem than you make it. Unfortunately some parents make it an issue far out of proportion to its importance. Parents should try to remember that their reaction to a lover is likely to help or harm their child, not the lover.

Some gay children will actively avoid introducing a lover for fear that the parents will react in openly hostile ways. They are sometimes right, even though these parents cause more harm by their hostility. There are other gays who want their parents to meet a lover long before the parents feel ready for the experience.

One thing you can be certain of, everyone is anxious. Therefore it is advisable for you and your son or daughter to discuss the meeting before it occurs. In all probability you are all worried about the reactions of all the parties, and it is best to talk about some of your fears beforehand. It should also be obvious that the lover has something to say about this meeting as well. S/he may not be interested in meeting you at all. S/he may believe that only harm can result from such a meeting, and this may reflect his or her own family relationship. If you really want to understand what a gay relationship is like, you will be wise to give priority to the lover's feelings over your own. After all, s/he is the outsider in your family, and faces the problems any outsider would when a love relationship develops. Homosexuality just emphasizes these problems and introduces some new ones.

There are a number of ways that parents push their children away because of hostile reactions to a lover. One of the commonest is to say disparaging things about the lover in the presence of the gay. Perhaps their hope is that if they can wean their child from the lover, they might wean him or her from homosexuality. Most often the gay son or daughter resents the manipulation, and the blatant attempt to interfere in the relationship. The likely reaction is less contact with the parents, and defensiveness in whatever contact is left.

Condescension is another expression of hostility that should be avoided. Some parents may try to bend over backward to demonstrate how liberal they are. They put on a mask of approval, and the child and the lover see through it easily.

A third error is for one of the parents to meet the lover and to hide this fact from the other. This is sometimes done because the other parent "wouldn't approve." One parent should not deceive the other. It is an obvious form of hostility, and it will be resented by everyone, including the gay child.

The Carltons accepted Teddy's lover into their family. Some parents are able to do this; others are not. If you want to understand more about gay relationships and what it means to your child to have a lover, then you are bound to want to meet and get to know the lover. You should do this when you feel ready to do it, and not before. The time and place of the meeting should be discussed with your gay child.

Many parents need time to get used to the idea of meeting a lover, and they should take as much time as they need. Even if the first meeting doesn't go very well, there is always the opportunity for further meetings.

Sometimes a gay child will refuse to introduce a lover to his/her parents. If that happens it probably means that your child is afraid of rejection and wants to avoid the scene. If you would not be rejecting, then you should say so. If you think you might, wait for another day when your attitudes may change.

I believe that meeting a lover can be one of the most valuable experiences parents can have. It may be difficult, for just as parents feel a sense of loss when their heterosexual children get married, they may experience the same sense of loss when a gay child develops a love relationship. While such parents may protest that they object to the homosexuality, they may really be reacting to the fact that their child has grown up and is making an independent life. It may not be homosexuality, but the feeling that they are losing their child.

It is best that we face our fears. Most of the time our fears create more trouble and worry than the reality of a situation. If you have trusted your child in the past, if you have faith in his character, then you need not worry about his choice of a love partner. It's probably been a good choice. And even if his choice has been a poor one, he needs the freedom to make his own errors, just as you did in the past. We cannot protect our children, but we can allow them the opportunity to experience the world and make their own decisions.

Many parents worry about what happens in gay relationships. They believe that gays can never establish

lasting relationships. This is untrue. There are gay couples that have lived together for many years. There are
couples who have weathered the most severe problems
of discrimination through the years and still enjoy an
intimacy and closeness that might be a model for us all.
There are also some gay relationships that break up very
quickly. Sometimes the partners are sexually excited with
each other for a while and when the sex dies down so
does the relationship. Sometimes the couple cannot with-
stand the conflicts that occur in all close living. Sometimes they cannot stand the feeling of intimacy.

Except for the problems of discrimination, there
really aren't many differences between the lives of gay
couples and heterosexually married couples. Married
couples break up because the sexual desire becomes
satiated, or because they cannot deal with conflict. A
relationship between two people will last if they learn
how to share their lives together. A person's character is
far more important than his sexual preference.

Most of us do not come from families where
communication is so clear and love so abundant as in the
Carlton family. One of the reasons Teddy's homosexuality was not threatening to them was that there were so few
feelings of resentment from child-raising problems in the
past. In many other families homosexuality is identified
as the issue but older problems smolder underneath.
When this is the case, a child's homosexuality can at first
create distance between the family members. But even
this can be used to advantage. Distance between family
members can mobilize people to straighten out old
family problems. If family members can face events of
the past, communication can be reestablished. This has
happened in many families in which the homosexuality
of a child has stimulated parents to talk to each other and
try to heal old wounds. More than one family has become
more secure in its relationships because of a crisis. Many

families are only a short step away from the unity of the Carltons, but to get there takes some strength and willingness to listen, and perhaps to feel hurt. Perhaps it boils down to whether or not a family and its members want to know the truth about each other, and whether they feel the truth will make them stronger.

chapter seven

THE FRIEDMAN FAMILY

Marvin Friedman was sitting in the synagogue. It was one of the high holy days. The Friedmans were Orthodox Jews and had long cultivated a tradition of religious scholarship. Most of the male members of the family had been rabbis. Marvin, as the firstborn in his family, was expected to continue the tradition. He had already been studying at the yeshiva for ten years, and he attended willingly.

When Marvin put a skullcap on his head and his prayer shawl around his shoulders he did so with a profound feeling of oneness with God. The rules of tradition gave Marvin a sense of structure that he needed badly in his life.

When Marvin entered the synagogue that day he was looking forward to the service and the opportunity to show his father how far he had progressed in his religious studies.

As Marvin sat down, wrapped in the prayer shawl his father had given him for his bar mitzvah, a middle-aged man who seldom came to the weekly services sat beside him. Marvin took no special note of him at first, but during the service he gradually became aware of the man's physical closeness. If he had been anywhere else Marvin would have sensed what was about to happen.

After about fifteen minutes the man began to rub his knee against Marvin's. Getting no response, the man placed his hand on Marvin's knee and began to stroke it. Marvin couldn't believe this was happening. It seemed so completely impossible that he was momentarily paralyzed. He stared at his knee and at the man's hand. Only when the man began to move his hand toward Marvin's thigh did he realize what the man's intentions were.

Marvin's face flushed with anger. His whole body began to shake. With the greatest difficulty he controlled his impulse to attack the man. He pushed the hand off his leg and looked straight into the man's eyes with an expression of hatred and contempt. To use the service as a place to find sex was the lowest thing he could think of. He quickly moved to another seat and spent the rest of the service imagining the things he would do to this sacrilegious animal.

A cafeteria-style meal was provided after the service, and Marvin was one of the boys selected to serve. He dished out the food and waited for the man who had already become a hateful obsession. When he appeared, Marvin looked at him with the same burning anger as before. He threw a bare bone on the man's plate and yelled, "This is all you deserve, you dog!"

Mr. Friedman, who was standing nearby, couldn't believe what he saw and heard. A man with a hair-trigger temper, he ran over to his son and pulled him out of the serving area, out of the synagogue, and into the street. He began to hit the boy.

Marvin tried to hold his father's hands back as he attempted to tell him what had happened, hoping his father would understand. But Joshua Friedman was appalled at the story and refused to believe the boy. To him it was just another example of his son's disrespectfulness. He was incapable of seeing how upset the boy was, and how urgently Marvin wanted to talk to him.

Marvin would have told him everything that day. The incident at the synagogue was so unsettling that Marvin would have gladly confessed to his father the long series of homosexual episodes that had occupied so much of his time for the past two years. But Mr. Friedman continued to beat his son without mercy, until an uncle walked over and restrained him.

"It's enough," the uncle said. "He's only a boy."

The relationship between Marvin and his father had not always been so strained. At Marvin's birth Mr. Friedman had seen the opportunity to continue the family tradition of the firstborn son becoming a rabbi. Mr. Friedman was also a firstborn son but had not become a rabbi, and he had felt guilty about it. That burden began to lighten at Marvin's birth.

For the first seven years Mr. Friedman felt nothing but joy with his son. At an early age the boy began to receive religious instruction, first from his parents, and than at the yeshiva, where he was sent at the age of six. The family lived comfortably, and two more children were born, another boy and a girl.

Marvin identified with all the values of his father, particularly the religious ones. As a little boy, Marvin had only one problem with his father, and that was loneliness. Mr. Friedman owned a small business and was often away for weeks at a time. Mrs. Friedman's care could not alleviate Marvin's feeling of loss during these absences.

It was during one of these business trips that Marvin first slept with his father's picture. It became a habitual way of dealing with his loneliness. Marvin would take a framed picture of his father, put it under the pillow, and go to sleep. When he couldn't sleep he would look at the picture and that would calm him.

One night during one of these periods Marvin felt

particularly lonely. He looked at the picture of his father and cradled it in his arms, as if his father were in bed with him. He fell asleep and had a dream.

They were in bed together, and the father looked down at his son and smiled. The boy touched his father's face and then his hair. By an unspoken understanding the father did the same to him. They lay there touching each other in soft and affectionate ways for the next few minutes. Then the father looked at his son and said, "You're a good boy." And the two of them fell asleep in each other's arms.

When Marvin was eight years old his father's business failed. It was a tragic event for the Friedman family. Mr. Friedman was forced into bankruptcy and had to sell his house. They moved to a small apartment in a neighborhood Mr. Friedman felt was unworthy of his standing in the community.

Joshua Friedman had very strong beliefs about his responsibilities both as a man and as head of the family. Nothing was more central to these beliefs than his duty to provide a home for his wife and children. Failure to do so proved his incompetence as a man, as a husband, and as a father. The public disgrace of bankruptcy and the shame of needing help from his relatives were unendurable to a man whose standards of masculinity were so strict and demanding.

Mr. Friedman felt overpowered by guilt. Demons from his childhood reappeared and hounded him for previous failures. His failure to become a rabbi, the ways in which he had defied his own father, and his struggles in the business world, all combined to make him believe that his manhood was a sham. Nothing could diminish his self-hate, neither the care of his wife nor the helpfulness of his brothers. Indeed their concern was further proof to him of his incompetence and need for charity. His children's love could not console him, for it only served to remind him of his shortcomings.

At first Mr. Friedman felt depressed. Later a different and more permanent pattern set in. He became an angry and bitter man. Nowhere was this anger expressed so much as toward the children. When he looked at Marvin or his other children he saw only a reflection of his own shame. Their laughter and playfulness he felt as a reproach. When he looked at Marvin in particular, he was reminded of his feelings of failure. In his own eyes he had failed his firstborn son. For this reason he had to reject the boy.

His wife, Sarah Friedman, was unable to reason with her husband. Through years of experience she had learned that it was impossible to talk quietly with him when he was upset. In earlier years he had struck her if she attempted to interfere with his line of reasoning. She found that the only way to live with him was to submerge her own feelings and help him to do whatever he wanted. It was a compromise she made with herself in the belief that she could support either her husband or her children, but not both. She chose her husband and directed her energy to trying to get Marvin to conform to his father's wishes. Sarah believed that if she made Marvin conform, the family would regain their earlier happiness. But Marvin felt severely rejected by his father even when he tried to conform.

Joshua Friedman did not treat all his children the same. Especially during the period of his business failures he reacted quite differently to each of them. His daughter, the oldest child, was seldom criticized, probably because she was a daughter, and women were not a threat to his male image. Though he was cool toward her, he never abused her the way he did Marvin. The second son, Mark, four years younger than Marvin, looked up to his older brother. But he was confused by the harsh treatment Marvin received from his father. Wisely, he stayed out of his father's way because he saw the effects of the battles between Joshua and Marvin Friedman. Poor Mark always felt that he couldn't get along with both of them, and he became an unfortunate victim in the family war.

In the course of the next few years the distance between Mr. Friedman and his children became a complete severance. Marvin turned to his grandmother for the affection he did not receive at home. The boy spent long periods with the old woman, caring for her needs. Marvin would shop, cook and clean for his grandmother.

One day Marvin asked his parents about his grandmother's illness. To him it seemed to be getting worse. His parents told him that she only had a cold. In fact, she was dying of leukemia. Throughout that period Marvin helped his grandmother, never knowing that she had only a short time to live. Then one day the old woman wanted the boy to stay longer than he had planned, but he protested that he wanted to play with his friends and left. She died that weekend. Marvin was fourteen.

Six months later he had his first homosexual experience. Returning home from the yeshiva on the subway, Marvin noticed a middle-aged man sitting across from him. He found the man very attractive. Marvin became acutely aware of an erection and impulsively decided to follow him.

Marvin was quite direct about what he wanted from the man, who at first refused, frightened by Marvin's youth. But the boy would not be put off, and aggressively he pushed his way into the man's house. The man was not sexually excited by a boy so young, but he was impressed by the forcefulness with which Marvin entered. Almost instinctively, the man recognized that so

brazen an exterior must conceal fear of, as well as the
desire for, softness and affection. He placed his arm
around the boy's shoulder and they sat on the couch
together, the boy's head in his arms. Later on they went
to bed together.

From then on, Marvin looked for older men to
have sex with. During the summer he would cruise the
boardwalks, but during the rest of the year it was
subways. As we might expect, the orgasmic release was
of secondary importance to Marvin. He was seeking
affection, and as it was not forthcoming from his father,
he had to find other men to provide it.

His sexual fantasies were always the same. He
would imagine cuddling up close to an older man, the
man hugging and kissing him affectionately. They would
fondle each other, and the fantasy would end with the
two going to sleep together, their arms and legs wrapped
around each other as if they were one. Alone, Marvin
would masturbate to this fantasy. He directed his pick-
ups to do these things, and only then would he allow
them to have an orgasm. In those days, he seldom cared
whether he himself did. What was most important was
the feeling of being secure and wanted. Even as Marvin
got older and more experienced sexually, he preferred to
spend time with his partners, taking baths together, lying
on the floor without clothes and listening to records—and
forever touching each other.

At first Marvin was upset by the sweat and liquids
of the sexual encounters. Perhaps, too, the homosexual
realization bothered him, for sometimes he returned with
the feeling that his body was dirty. He would come home
and take a scalding shower. He would scrub his body
fiercely, a body that he felt had been contaminated by the
sexual act. After the shower he felt better.

Some men gave him money for doing things he
wanted to do, and Marvin accepted it. In the course of the
next two years Marvin had sex with many men, saving his

money for the day that he could afford his own apartment. About this time he made friends with a number of gay boys his own age.

One day one of these friends visited Marvin at home. Like Marvin, he was a teenager, and he was studying to be a dancer. He had started having homosexual experiences at an even earlier age than Marvin. The boy was quite comfortable with his homosexuality, and unconcerned about the attitudes of others.

Marvin felt afraid when his friend left the house. His father had become suspicious of Marvin's late-night activities, and Marvin was worried that his father might be starting to figure out what he was doing. He was quite right. Joshua Friedman had noticed the many phone calls that Marvin received, and particularly the calls from obviously older men. Marvin often left the house after these calls and wouldn't return until very late at night. After meeting this friend of his son, Mr. Friedman felt certain his fears were well grounded.

"This boy is a friend of yours?" asked Mr. Friedman.

"Yes, he's a friend of mine," said Marvin.

"This friend, is he a homosexual?"

"I don't know if he's a homosexual. How should I know?"

"Let me ask you another question. Are you a homosexual?"

"Why, because I have a friend who might be a homosexual?"

"This friend is a fag. You're a fag, too, aren't you?"

"What are you saying? Just because I have a friend who's a fag, you're calling me a fag?"

"You're a fag. I think you're crazy. I know what you do, and I think you're crazy. I'm going to call up the doctor and tell him you're a fag. I want you committed to an institution. You're no good anyway."

Marvin was very upset about this confrontation

and kept protesting that he wasn't a "fag." But his
father's voice drowned out the denials. "You're a fag!
You're a fag."

Marvin ran to his room and began to cry. He was
used to his father's anger and accusations. That was not
what bothered him. Even his homosexual guilt was not
the primary problem that day.

There had been so much stress in this family
on "being a man"; so much talk among his father and
his uncles about "faygelehs" and how they were like
women—weak and contemptible. For many years
Marvin had heard jokes about faygelehs and stories
about how any real man should treat them, with jeers and
contempt. Marvin became confused about his own masculinity. The myth that homosexual men are like women
dies very hard, especially in a society that uses guilt and
shame as tools of internal psychological control. In fact
there was no effeminacy in the boy, but reality was far
outweighed by fear, and his fear paralyzed him. Though
telling the truth to his father would not have changed his
ideas, it might have led the boy to more effective ways of
fighting the new challenge to his emotional stability, for
a very serious psychological war had just begun.

The night after Mr. Friedman called his son a
"fag," at the dinner table, he told of an occasion in his
youth when a gay man had tried to pick him up. Proudly
he told Marvin of punching the man in the face and
beating him to the ground. Marvin could see that his
father's anger over that event had not diminished over
the years. Marvin was shocked to see his father demonstrate with his arms how he had beaten the man, and to
hear the pride in his voice at the humiliation he had
brought upon him. Marvin was afraid that this anger
would be turned against him one day.

Then Mrs. Friedman went to work on Marvin. Her
style was different· While Mr. Friedman attacked the

boy, Mrs. Friedman used guilt and shame to try to make him change his behavior. She came into his room to tell him how much she cried every night "because of what you are." She told him over and over again that she couldn't tell anyone in the family about her "troubles," because of her shame. In fact, Marvin knew that she had already told everyone in the family. He was already a cause célèbre.

"Tomorrow, Marvin," Mrs. Friedman said, "I want you to go to your grandmother's grave. I want you to pray for her forgiveness because of what you are. Pray for her to help you so this horrible thing will go away. You know how she loved you and would do anything for you. Go, Marvin. If you pray hard enough, you can make it go away. Please do this. Do this for me and your father. We're suffering so much."

Mrs. Friedman cried as she said this, and Marvin felt every bit as guilty and hurt as he was supposed to feel. Just then his father, having overheard their discussion, entered the room angrily. He began to yell again, telling Marvin that his grandmother had hated him and had always hated him. "She knew you would become a queer. She told me. She knew since you were a child you'd turn out that way. That's why she was nice to you. She thought she could change you."

This was the most harmful thing ever said to Marvin. It wounded him deeply. It struck so sensitive a nerve that it left him completely defenseless. Marvin just sat there dazed. It wasn't until later that night that his mother told him that Mr. Friedman had lied. But it was already too late. He had no idea which one to believe.

Marvin reacted with bitterness toward his parents. From his point of view both of them had deceived and lied to him so often that he could think only of retribution. He devised a plan to get even with them. If his father hurt Marvin, then Marvin would hurt back, and he

would hit in a place where Mr. Friedman was most
sensitive, his masculinity. If Mr. Friedman feared that
Marvin would be "effeminate" then that's just what
Marvin would do. He decided to make all his father's
fears come true.

Marvin began to buy women's clothes, first a
dress, then shoes and a pocketbook. He was saving them
for his sister's wedding.

On the evening of the wedding Marvin arrived
wearing the clothes he had bought. He was dressed like
Bette Davis, with a wide-brimmed hat on his head and an
enormous cigarette holder in his hand. One can easily
imagine the shock that struck everyone in the room as he
entered the hall and walked to the middle of the floor.
Slinking in a caricature of a sexy woman, he stretched out
the hand with the long cigarette holder and said, "Anybody have a light?"

The hall was filled with his relatives, all of whom
had heard about the "Friedman troubles." Many of the
family were Hassidic Jews, and Marvin's costume must
have looked especially bizarre among the long black
clothes and long beards of the Hassids.

Marvin had every intention of humiliating his
father as his father had humiliated him. He succeeded
very well. Mrs. Friedman began to cry, but Mr. Friedman
remained impassive, giving no outward sign or reaction.
But his guts churned. For him this was the final degrada-
tion. Being publicly disgraced by his son was the final
blow to his self-esteem, and he plotted his revenge.

Marvin left the wedding early and went straight
home and to sleep. He was awakened by loud noise and
bright lights in the room, and opening his eyes, he saw
two policemen, a couple of men in white coats, and his
father. Mr. Friedman had called the police and told them
that Marvin had tried to kill him, and both the police and
an ambulance from the local hospital had come to the
house. They ordered Marvin to get dressed, though he

protested that he was innocent of the changes. Marvin was placed in the ambulance and strapped into a stretcher, his father sitting to one side.

Marvin was admitted to the hospital for observation as a mental patient. As the doctors opened the big iron doors, Marvin turned to his father and said, "Well, I hope you're satisfied, Mr. Friedman. You'll never see your son again."

Mr. Friedman began to cry at this, and Marvin's anger abated somewhat. Bad as he was feeling for himself that night, he felt as bad for his father. Marvin was released within a week.

Soon after this tragic event, Mr. Friedman died. Many people in the family said that Marvin had killed his father bit by bit each day. At the funeral Marvin stood next to his sister, whose relationship with his father had been less tempestuous than his. At the end of the service they walked together to the car. His sister was still crying, but Marvin's eyes were dry. "I can't remember a bad thing he ever did," she said, and Marvin replied, "That's funny. I can't remember a good thing he ever did."

It was a long drive home, and the two of them sat quietly, deep in their own thoughts. Marvin wondered at his sister's comment about his father's goodness. How different it was for him. He could remember only the many nights of fighting, the terrible arguments, the accusations made against him, and the humiliations of many years.

Then suddenly Marvin noticed that they were passing the old synagogue he had attended as a little boy. He remembered a friend's bar mitzvah. Some of the women had bought lots of candy bars for the kids. They sat in the balcony waiting for the right moment to shower them upon the children, who were sitting anxiously below.

Mr. Friedman saw that time coming and led

Marvin to a place directly underneath the gallery. Marvin could see a gleam in his father's eyes. He told his son to help him spread his prayer shawl like a big net, and the two of them waited for the rain of candy. Suddenly the shower of candy bars fell from above, landing neatly in the net the Friedmans had prepared. The two grabbed handfuls of candy and dropped the rest to the floor. Then they ran out of the synagogue and into their car. Mr. Friedman watched his son's laughter and happiness as he gobbled down candy bars at a rate Mrs. Friedman would never have allowed.

This memory, lost for so long, led to others that had been buried under years of anger and fighting. They were of better days for Marvin and his father. Marvin began to relax just a little bit.

chapter eight

THE FRIEDMAN FAMILY REVISITED

Most families are not as troubled as the Friedmans. The mistakes they made are no different from the mistakes made by most families, only here they are more dramatically illustrated. Unfortunately there are a large number of families that avoid coming to grips with their problems by hurting each other. Let us attempt to reconstruct the complicated relationship between Mr. Friedman and his son Marvin.

Let's look at Mr. Friedman first. How can we make sense out of all the harmful things Mr. Friedman did to both himself and his son? Think of yourself and your own experiences as a parent. It may help you to understand this family a little better.

When you act like a loving father or mother, your child responds like a loving child. But there may be other times when you think only about yourself. Perhaps, like Mr. Friedman, you have financial problems, or have had a quarrel with your spouse, or another child is ill. For whatever reason, you have less patience than usual. You become short-tempered and judgmental. You may punish the child, sometimes unreasonably, though you may regret your actions later. All parents do this. None of us can be loving parents all the time. We have our own personal problems, to say nothing of the problems we have in raising and supporting a family. All parents get angry some of the time, and when it is only some of the time, it doesn't hurt the children.

However, when a parent acts angry most of the time, the child has no choice but to respond with anger.

Sometimes we act like loving parents, and at other times we act like angry parents. This is the key to understanding what happened in the Friedman family. Only if we can distinguish between Mr. Friedman's behavior as the *loving father* and as the *angry father* can we make sense out of their family conflict. Marvin's behavior represented either the *loving son* or the *angry son*. I am suggesting that a person can sometimes act as if he were two different people, one warm and understanding, the other cold and harsh.

In effect, Mr. Friedman was two different men. The first Mr. Friedman was the father of Marvin's early childhood, a man who loved his son and cared for his needs. This was the loving father in Marvin's life. Marvin reacted as a loving son, identified with his father's values, and returned the affection he received.

After Mr. Friedman's business failure everything changed dramatically. As his own personal troubles grew, he began to act in a way contrary to his earlier behavior. His troubles overwhelmed his early love, and he turned into an angry father. He became a father who heard only the voice of his own sadness and guilt, and was deaf to the pleas of his family to listen to their voices as well. Part of Mr. Friedman's change was to reject Marvin by treating him as the bad son.

In so doing, Mr. Friedman helped to create the bad son. When we treat our children as "bad," we show them that we expect them to act that way. Then when we demand that they change their behavior and act "good" it rarely works.

Children invariably obey our expectations, not our demands. Children sense what we expect of them, and it makes no difference whether the expectation is positive or negative. What we expect, they deliver, regardless of what we say we want.

Mr. Friedman expected Marvin to act in ways that he would not approve. So Marvin gave his father exactly what he expected. In a psychological sense, Marvin was fulfilling his father's request, as he had always tried to do. By acting as the bad son, Marvin continued to show his love for his father. This must sound like a crazy statement. Let's see if it is.

Mr. Friedman was a man in extreme pain. He considered himself a failure as a man, as a businessman, and as a father. How could he live under these conditions? How long can a person survive when his self-esteem has been shattered so completely? The only alternative, for him, was to transform his depression into anger. He needed some way to increase his self-esteem, and the easiest way to effect this was by blaming another person. If we can blame someone for what *they do*, it keeps our mind off the things that *we do*. Blaming Marvin made Mr. Friedman feel stronger, and strength was necessary for his survival.

By playing the bad son, Marvin helped his father's emotional stability. Marvin became the focus of his father's attention once again, taking Mr. Friedman's mind off himself. When he worried about Marvin and got angry at Marvin's behavior, Mr. Friedman could feel that his son was harming him, and then he was less depressed. It is very possible that Marvin's humiliating conduct and his desire to obey his father's expectations may actually have saved his father's life. If Marvin had not responded as the bad son, Mr. Friedman might have continued to move deeper into his depression.

Marvin used his homosexuality as a weapon to

hurt his father, just as his father expected him to do. Mr. Friedman could then see himself as the victim of some-one else, who was purposely trying to hurt him. Someone else could share some of the blame. Who better than his firstborn son?

Was either Marvin or his father aware of this conspiracy to remove some of the father's guilt? Not likely. But members of a family most often help each other in ways they do not understand. Family members often have the ability to sense the others' private needs although these are never discussed. Family members play roles that help maintain the psychological stability of the others, no matter what the risks to themselves. This was the case with Mr. Friedman and Marvin. The boy played a special role in the family, a kind of "chosen one" whose singular responsibility was to relieve the pain of his father's existence by taking it upon his own shoulders.

Mr. Friedman was obsessed with proving his masculinity, and he had very specific criteria for mascu-line success. A man makes a good living for his wife and family; a man has a good home in a good neighborhood; a man can control his children and this is demonstrated by their adherence to his values; a man can take care of his own problems, financial and personal; a man teaches his family to carry on the family traditions; a man has sons who hold the same idea of what it means to be a man.

To someone like Mr. Friedman, failure to live up to *all* these demands is prima facie evidence of *failure as a man*. When Mr. Friedman's business failed, it was not a business failure to him but a personal one, a masculine failure. Under these conditions, life became a series of battles, in which victory is never possible and all failures are catastrophic. Regardless of what others may have thought of Mr. Friedman, he demanded the most irrational and inhuman standard of himself. The pain he inflicted on others was slight when compared with the torture he inflicted upon himself.

Thus it was his sense of guilt that became the crucial motivation in all his actions toward his family, and that is primarily responsible for the tragedy of the Friedman family. It explains why father and son could never talk together as reasonable people.

Mr. Friedman was a man who had no independent standards of behavior. He always needed to live up to some external criterion, especially regarding masculinity. He never felt an internal sense of his own competence, but measured it always in terms of externals: children, or money, or status.

"Like father, like son"? Indeed, yes. Marvin, the firstborn son, became an important extension of Mr. Friedman's ego, and his responsibility was to amend all the errors that his father had made in his own lifetime. The boy would be the rabbi his father had failed to become; the boy would be the scholar his father had not become; the boy would become the "strong man" his father had not been.

But most important, Marvin learned his father's ideas of reward. Rewards were external; they represented approval from other people. Marvin very early became dependent upon his father for approval, and no one else could provide it. Naturally all children need approval, but Marvin was never taught to develop his own standards. This was the reason that Marvin felt so deserted when his father left on business trips. He would only accept approval from his father, not his mother.

In character and personality, father and son were reflected images of one another. Like father, the boy was in conflict about what it meant to be a man. His homosexuality was particularly troublesome since he had been taught that "fags" were effeminate, "queers" were sissies, "homos" were worse than women. He felt he was all these things.

Marvin felt guilty that he had not become the "man" his father had wanted. Just as the father felt guilty that he had disappointed his son, so the son felt guilty that he had disappointed the father. Thus guilt became as prominent in the son's life as in the father's, and both distracted themselves from their guilt by the same means: getting angry with someone else. Marvin's violent reaction to the man in the synagogue was in part an instance of this, and his fury was an indication of how much guilt he felt. Mr. Friedman's reaction to Marvin's behavior in the cafeteria line demonstrated the same instant rage.

How did Marvin feel about his homosexuality? There are clear indications that he was guilty and ashamed, as, for example, in his reactions to sex. He felt "dirty" after having sex with a man, and felt the need to take a shower to cleanse himself. However, most of the time Marvin was probably unaware of how he felt about being a homosexual. What happens with a young man like this is that, instead of experiencing the distress of his guilt, he impulsively attacks another person, and by so doing avoids his own sense of guilt. I suggest that Marvin felt doubly guilty, as a poor representative of a man, and as a homosexual. Recognizing this would have thrown him into a serious depression.

Father and son were alike in other ways as well. When hurt, they would avoid feelings of pain and sorrow by striking out against the offending party. They would embarrass the other person, humiliate the other person, find something that person believed and destroy it. If the father was a man who questioned his own masculinity, then Marvin would do everything he could to remind his father of it, and for the *coup de grâce* he would announce it publicly. At the wedding he humiliated his father. The father had already done the same to him at the synagogue and, later, when he had lied and told the boy that his grandmother hated him.

It became a war between the *angry father* and the *angry son,* and homosexuality was the pretext upon which this war was waged. Each time one of them touched the other's sense of failed masculinity, a new battle was fought—a battle that neither could win because the real struggles were internal ones.

Was homosexuality a real issue? Not in the conventional sense. One can easily assume that no one in the family, perhaps not even Marvin, understood the meaning of homosexuality as loving and caring for another man as a mature person. In part, Mr. Friedman attacked homosexuals because of his religious beliefs, but these were of secondary importance. The social meaning of homosexuality was the primary motivation for his reaction. A homosexual was not a man, and that was cause enough for discomfort.

And what of Mrs. Friedman? In some ways she seems a perfect match for her husband. As he is motivated by guilt, she motivates through guilt, using it to control people. She showed this quite well when she asked Marvin to pray for forgiveness at his grandmother's grave. He was confused enough, but when Mrs. Friedman brought in the name of the dead grandmother, she wounded the boy. To her it must have been only another way to use guilt to control her son, but for Marvin it was an attack upon the only constructive family relationship he had ever had.

Guilt is one of the primary tools that families use to control their members. When a child becomes too old to punish, many families use guilt as a replacement. It works only too well. It's possible to control another person's behavior by picking out a weakness, making the person feel guilty about it, and playing on that guilt to get the person to do what is wanted. But guilt is an insidious tool, because it can, and usually does, rebound on everyone in the family.

There are two kinds of guilt. One kind is *self-guilt,* the guilt we feel for having done something that we feel is wrong. It may or may not be expressed to another person; it originates in our own conscience. The crucial thing about *self-guilt* is that it serves *our need* to be honest, not the need to conform to another person's demands.

The second kind of guilt is very different. Let's call it *controlling guilt.* That's when another person decides that your behavior is wrong and does everything possible to make you feel guilty. If you can be made to feel guilty, then the other person will be in a better position to force you to change your behavior.

Unfortunately, controlling guilt is used extensively in families where there is a gay child, and it usually becomes a spiderweb that eventually entangles the whole family. If parents use it with a child, the child is likely to retaliate with "guilt attacks" against the parents. Siblings and other family members are involved as well. After a while the attacks and counterattacks can devastate everyone.

There are a number of techniques of using controlling guilt, but all of them follow a general principle. The guilt attack begins with the statement by word or deed: "*I am suffering.*"

The parent is saying, "Look how bad I am feeling. Look how distressed I am now that this thing has happened." The parent of the homosexual indicates a change in his or her behavior that is directly linked to the child's homosexuality. It is crucial that the parent appear to suffer.

The second step is: "*You have done this to me.*"

It is absolutely required that a parent who wants to

control a son or daughter through guilt indicate that the parent's suffering is entirely the fault of the child. "If not for you, I would be a happy person" is the theme. The parents are adamantly rejecting the idea that each person is responsible for his own suffering, that one does it to oneself. It is crucial at this stage of the process to make everyone believe that the child is attacking the parent, not the other way around. If the parent can do this, the child is ready for the final step: "*If you really loved me, you would change.*"

How ironic that "love" should be the key word to controlling someone. In effect, the parent says, "By doing this thing, you show that you no longer love me, and that's why I am in so much pain. If you really loved me, you wouldn't hurt me so. The only way you can show me that you love me is by changing your behavior. Then I'll know that you really love me, and I can show my love to you."

Sometimes a child's behavior can be controlled by this device of equating love for you with doing what you want. It's a very powerful technique, and when used consistently can actually force a child to behave differently. Under extraordinary circumstances you might even get a child to stop having homosexual experiences, though you will not remove the desire to have them. But a price must be paid for controlling through guilt, and it's a heavy one. While a child may change his/her behavior because of controlling guilt, s/he will also come to resent the person who invoked the guilt. If the struggle has been intense, as in the Friedman family, resentment may develop into hatred. The person who has been made to feel guilty knows that s/he has lost control of his/her own behavior. S/he will resent your power and his/her own loss of power. We love when we feel free to love, not when we are forced to. The person who changes his or her behavior because of controlling guilt comes to feel self-hatred for doing so, and to distrust, if not actively hate, the person who made him or her feel powerless.

If you control someone by guilt, you must be prepared to have that person mistrust your every action. Everything you do will be interpreted as further evidence that you wish to make him or her powerless. Protection against feelings of guilt and powerlessness will become the most important psychological need. The child may become secretive and aloof. S/he may learn to lie and cheat. If things get bad enough—and by that I mean, if s/he feels guilty or angry enough—s/he may leave the family, not just physically, but psychologically as well. It's possible for a child to disown his or her family.

It happens in many families, as in the Friedman family, that everyone carries his resentment and guilt to the grave. When people are resentful, they feel hurt. But the family that uses guilt as a tool of control cannot express their hurt for fear that that too will be used against them. So the hurt remains like a time bomb, ready to go off whenever the "guilt button" is pressed.

How can you tell whether you are using guilt to hurt your child? Like so many things, it's easy to see in other people but not so easy to see in yourself. If you tell someone that you have become ill because of his or her behavior, you're using guilt. If you tell him or her that your wife or husband or anyone else is suffering *because of* his or her behavior, you're using guilt; when you say that you're so embarrassed about that behavior that you can't tell anyone about it, you're using guilt. And most harmful of all, if you change your behavior drastically, become depressed or hostile and refuse to discuss it, when your child knows it has to do with his or her homosexuality, you're using guilt. Whenever you tell your child that your hurt is his or her fault, you are using guilt.

Our society has so encouraged the use of guilt in families that it has become a very hard job for parents to distinguish between *feeling guilty* and *using guilt to control a child.* But please remember this—whenever you use guilt you hurt your own son or daughter, and what hurts your child will ultimately hurt you as well.

There was a moment, just one, when Marvin and his father might have transcended their attacks upon each other. There was a moment when Mr. Friedman could have stopped hurting his son and himself. There was just one moment when their defenses were down and their hurt began to show through. That was the day Mr. Friedman had his son sent to the mental hospital. When Marvin said, "Well, I hope you're satisfied, Mr. Friedman. You'll never see your son again," and the father began to cry, Marvin felt sorry for him. They were both in pain and showed it. If only they had responded to their pain and reached out for one another, they might have resolved their troubles. In that brief moment they could have recaptured some of the love of the early years. If only they could have taken that step, Mr. Friedman would have become a happier man, and his son would not still be looking for the "good father." For the Friedmans it must now remain "if only. . . ." For other families the chance is still there.

chapter nine

THE BROWNE FAMILY

Ann Simmons did not want to see her parents suffer any more. During the past year their pain had been unbearable to watch. Any mention of Cathy, the youngest daughter, was enough to bring tears to her father's eyes. He cried constantly, as if his daughter were dead. Mrs. Browne dealt with the problem by complete denial. To her this was only a phase her twenty-six-year-old daughter was going through. She refused to discuss the truth of what had happened. Worst of all, Mrs. Browne continued to maintain that her poor husband would die from this "terrible thing."

Ann, four years older than Cathy, had no difficulty accepting her sister's lesbianism, nor did her husband. Cathy had always impressed Ann as being different, though she had never suspected that her sister would become a lesbian. But Cathy, who had divorced her husband and moved to the West Coast, sounded happy with her homosexuality and her lesbian friends. The move had left Ann and her husband to deal with the problems of her parents, who were extremely confused. Like many other people, they had thought that a married woman couldn't become a lesbian. To them Cathy's marriage was a sure sign that she was a "normal girl."

The marriage lasted two and a half years; Cathy became aware of her homosexual feelings, and the marriage ended.

Ann had heard about an organization in New York City called the Parents of Gays, started by a group of parents whose children were homosexual. The parents met each month to talk about how they were affected by the homosexuality of their children. Other parents heard about the group, and slowly it began to grow. Ann hoped that these parents might be able to help her own. Ann herself couldn't; they just wouldn't talk to her. Ann was eager to go to a meeting. She loved her sister and wanted to learn more about lesbianism so that she could understand Cathy's life a little better. She also knew that her parents desperately needed help, and that was her primary reason for taking action.

Although they resisted the idea, Mr. and Mrs. Browne agreed to go to a meeting; but Ann took no chances. She decided to stay at her parents' house Saturday night and drive them into New York City for the meeting the next day. If they balked at the last minute, she wanted to be there to fight it. She knew how often they went back on their word.

Three weeks before, she had given her parents the brochure for Parents of Gays. At first her mother said she would think about going, then later she said she'd go. But Mrs. Browne added, "But why do you have to go, Ann? It says Parents of Gays, not sisters of gays."

"Look, Mama, we're a family. Let's do this together. Maybe Paul should go too. After all, he's Cathy's brother. At least we three will go and we'll talk about it and work it out among ourselves."

But trouble started on Saturday night. Mrs. Browne decided that she wouldn't go. "I never said I was going and I'm not going."

"You've got to be kidding. What are you talking about? Didn't you tell Daddy and me that you were going?"

"I never said anything like that. I don't want to be pressured into this thing. I'm not ready for this. I've got too many problems."

"Look, Mama, you don't want to go to the meeting because you'll have to admit that your daughter is a lesbian and you don't want to do that. And if you go to the meeting you may find out that it's all right to be a lesbian and that other parents love their children no matter what. That's why you don't want to go. You still want to believe that Cathy's going to find another man and marry him. It's not going to happen, Mama."

"Look, you never know. Who knows what's going to be?"

"What are you talking about? Anything that's going to be is going to be with another woman. It's not going to be with some guy."

"What do you know about it?"

"Daddy's coming to the meeting. He told me tonight that he wants to go."

"Well, if he thinks this is good for him, then he can go. But I'm not going."

Ann went to sleep that evening confident that at least her father would go to the meeting and find some sympathetic people to talk to. But things were worse in the morning.

Ann and her husband were at the breakfast table with her younger brother and her mother. Her father was sitting in the den; he didn't want any breakfast. Ann thought this was only an indication of his nervousness about the meeting. She saw that he was wearing dungarees and a flannel shirt, unusual attire for him when he was going out somewhere, but she thought little about it.

Noticing the time, Ann went into the den to tell her

father that they would have to leave soon. Her father was crying.

"Look, Ann, I was up all last night thinking about this. Your mother and I have always done things together. I guess we're very lucky. We never had much money, but we always had each other. Whenever there's been a problem, or whenever something good happened, we've always been there together. We're partners, and if your mother's not ready to go, I don't think I should go either. Mother said maybe she would go next month, and if I've waited this long I can wait another month."

Ann returned to the kitchen knowing exactly why her father had changed his mind. Her mother was the culprit. It was an old tradition in the family for Mrs. Browne to make decisions for her husband while claiming that they were his. This clandestine technique of decision-making was always carried on out of sight of the children, who would have pointed out immediately how browbeaten their father was. Ann confronted her mother about it.

"You know Daddy's not going because of you."

"But, Ann, I can't make him do anything he doesn't want to."

"Daddy says he's going to wait until next month when he can go with you, because you're not ready to go now."

"And who knows how I'll feel next month? Who knows if I'll go at all?" This last comment was clearly a tactical error on Mrs. Browne's part. Ann rushed back into the den.

"Daddy, I just want to tell you that Mama said she doesn't know if she's going next month or any other month. She says there are too many things on her mind. So why don't you get together with her and find out what's going on in her mind."

Mr. Browne entered the kitchen and asked that he

and his wife be left alone to talk. The others left, and
standing outside the door they could hear the muffled
sound of their parents talking. The children had always
been angered by their parents' private conversations.
All their lives they had been excluded—and often
manipulated—by this tactic. Ann could hear her father
say, "Rose, I would give ten years of my life if Cathy
would go back to her husband."

Mrs. Browne jumped at the opportunity. She emphasized her own problems and how their daughter's
behavior had made things so embarrassing for them.
"Why should we talk to other people about this thing? I
don't want to show people my shame."

Ann was not going to allow her mother to control
her father this way. She went into the kitchen.

'Look, Daddy, we agreed this is not Cathy's problem. She's happy. We agreed it's our problem. Come on,
we'll go together. If Mama doesn't want to go, that's her
problem." The push from Ann was all that was needed,
and Mr. Browne went upstairs to change his clothes.
When he came down, he got into Ann's car and they
drove to the city.

Ann wondered why her parents had developed a
marital style of reinforcing each other's fears instead of
providing strength for each other. That's what had happened in the kitchen. Rose Browne had wanted to hide
"her shame," and her husband had said he would give
"ten years of my life." Instead of one parent helping the
other to face a problem constructively, the Brownes had
helped each other to feel victimized in the face of a
problem they did not understand. It was the communication problem between Mr. and Mrs. Browne that caused
them to feel helpless, not the lesbianism of their daughter.

During the hour's drive Ann thought more about
her family. Rose Browne was clearly the fulcrum of

power. She had a way of being the family switchboard through whom all information was forced to pass. She was particularly skillful at forming pacts of secrecy with first one member of the family, then another. Most often it was with one of the children, hiding some piece of information from her husband. She probably would have seen keeping secrets not as aggressive acts against her husband, but as a way of protecting him or one of the children. When she was buying a pair of shoes for one of them she would say, "Don't tell your father. He'll be angry if he knows how much they cost." Later the secrets included other people. "Don't tell . . . don't tell . . ."

How did Mr. Browne feel about these things? To learn, one would have to ask his wife. She was always the one who told the children what their father thought about things. Whenever one of the children did something that Mrs. Browne disliked, she would immediately accuse the child of trying to hurt their father. Cathy, the lesbian, was now spared this motherly manipulation, since she was three thousand miles away. It was the other children who were made to suffer. She even claimed that they were as distressed as she about her daughter, when clearly this was not the case.

Mr. Browne's difficulty in dealing with his family was different. He had been a working man all his life. Now, at the age of sixty-five, he had retired. He had had very little education, never going beyond the sixth grade. When he married he wanted his children to have a proper education, and he provided that education for them. Both his daughters had completed college, and his son would also go to college in a few years.

Children don't often understand how an uneducated parent can feel about their college education. Some parents are simply intimidated. Mr. Browne was like that. He never thought of himself as a smart man. Seeing how smart his children were, he became frightened at what he thought was his lack of intelligence. The smarter his kids got, the more he thought he was stupid. He wanted to ask questions about homosexuality, but he didn't know what to ask, or whom to ask. He wanted to confide in his oldest daughter, but he felt that would be a violation of his wife's confidence. He was caught in a vise; on one side was his sense of himself as an uneducated man, and on the other his conflicting loyalties to his children and his wife. The conflict was so great that he did nothing except cry from time to time. At least it relieved the pressure for a while.

Ann and her father talked little on the way to the meeting. It was clear to Ann that her father preferred silence and she didn't mind. She was thinking about her sister.

To those familiar with the lives of lesbians, there was nothing unusual about Cathy's experience. She had always been a woman who fully enjoyed sex. In her early years her sexual experiences with men were satisfying, and she had always been orgasmic with them.

At twenty-two she decided to marry a man whose interests in the arts were similar to her own. Sex was satisfying with him as well. She had not yet had any sexual experiences with women.

For Cathy it began with her interest in painting. She admired the bodies of women who looked particularly attractive to her, but it was an esthetic appeal, detached from any feelings of sexuality. In time she became friendly with a lesbian in her building, and sexual fantasies began intruding themselves into Cathy's thoughts. She wasn't quite sure what to make of them. On the one hand she knew that she was "straight." She slept with men and had sex with them. On the other hand she fantasized about having sex with women. She wondered if she could be bisexual.

Her relationship with the lesbian in the building

became more intimate. It was not the lesbian who encouraged this state of affairs, but Cathy. Cathy decided to seduce the lesbian. She still felt heterosexual because she was married. One day she pretended to be ill and asked the woman if she could stay in her apartment awhile. An hour later she had her first lesbian experience. It was the most thrilling she had ever had.

Lying in bed with her female companion, she thought how exciting it had been. But then she wondered what this revelation would mean in her life, for she was becoming aware that her true sexual desires were for women, not men. She realized too that her feelings for this woman went beyond orgasmic release. She was falling in love with her, and it was a love that was far more satisfying than anything she had experienced with her husband. She knew even then that she would ultimately live with a woman.

Cathy told her husband about her experience and he took it badly. She felt that he should know why her feelings toward him had changed so dramatically, and she didn't want him to suppose that he had done anything wrong. She just couldn't stay with him any more; she loved a woman. There aren't many men who are prepared to handle this kind of situation. A husband might be prepared to hear that his wife is seeing another man, and he might be prepared for the competition, but how does he compete with another woman?

He responded with anger, not wanting his wife to see how hurt he really was. He threw Cathy out of the house and told her never to come back. Cathy felt very guilty about what had happened, as if she had betrayed her husband. Cathy decided that she needed some space in which to live her life without her angry husband or her controlling family. She decided that she would give up her recent lesbian affair and move to another city. She chose San Francisco, where gay people seemed to lead a more relaxed life than in the community she came from.

Cathy had no intention of allowing her parents to interfere in her life. First she told her sister about her lesbianism, and Ann took the disclosure in stride. Then she went to see her parents and told them that she had left her husband and why. When her father began to cry and her mother dismissed the affair as a passing phase, Cathy left the house.

Ann knew most of this, and she tried not to resent Cathy's leaving her with the burden of trying to help her parents. Ann's car approached the church where the meeting was to take place. It was two forty-five and the meeting was scheduled to begin at three o'clock. After she parked the car Ann and her father walked into the church building and down a flight of stairs, into a large, brightly lit room. About twenty people were already there. Father and daughter sat in a far corner and waited for the meeting to begin.

chapter ten

THE PARENTS OF
GAYS MEETING

The Metropolitan Duane Church stands on the corner of 7th Avenue and 12th Street. Here, at three P.M. on the last Sunday of each month, Parents of Gays holds its monthly meeting. Parents of Gays was begun just a couple of years ago by a few parents who had read the awful books and heard the awful stories about how parents are to blame for their children's homosexuality, and thus for their dire misfortune. Parents of Gays helps parents learn about the significance of homosexuality in the family, and serves as a guide for maintaining family unity. There are now Parents of Gays groups in a number of cities around the country.

The Steering Committee met at two o'clock. Many letters had come in from parents around the country, and each had to be answered by one of the parents on the committee. There were also two speaking invitations, one from a local theological seminary and the other from a local college. Both groups wanted to hear how parents feel about homosexuality. A couple of weeks before, representatives of Parents of Gays had been invited to appear on a TV talk show, and many parents with gay children had called or written, wanting to know more about the group. The Steering Committee expected a heavy turn-out at today's meeting.

Some of the founders were at the committee meeting. They have kindly allowed me to use their real names. One was Jeannie Manford, the mother of Morty Manford, a gay liberationist from New York. Mr. and Mrs. Manford were among the first couples to come out publicly in support of their son and the civil rights of gay people. Just a few years ago they had been the only parents to march in the Gay Liberation Day parade, carrying a sign stating that their son was gay. Ten thousand gay people marched in that parade, and every one of them saw this middle-aged couple who walked the long route with their son. To the Manfords it had always been a matter of civil rights, and they decided to stand with their son and his friends to fight the prejudice against homosexuals. They believed that heterosexual people should stand up for the rights of gays, and they felt that public family support was the best way they could help. They hoped that their public stand would encourage other parents to join the struggle. Their tactics were successful, and other parents did.

Sarah Montgomery was another member of the Steering Committee. At seventy-eight she was still active in the civil rights movement, and she took more than her share of the letters to be answered that month. To Sarah Parents of Gays was not merely another civil rights organization. She had suffered as great a tragedy as any parent can experience.

Fifteen years before, her son had revealed his homosexuality to her. At that time homosexuality was still viewed as a perversion, and the laws of every state condemned homosexuals as criminals. Indeed, in some states homosexuals were punished with a prison sentence longer than that given to murderers. There were no gay liberation organizations; there was no thought that homosexuals had a right to be protected from discrimination and blackmail. It was the heyday of the police "entrapment" squads. "Entrapment" refers to the police practice of trying to entice a gay man into a sexual scene with a police officer who pretends to be a homosexual looking for sex. The youngest and most attractive officers would dress in tight-fitting pants and go to the places where gay men looked for sex. They participated in the sexual scenes as fully as any of the homosexuals present. Then they would flash their badges and arrest the men for indecency. In many cases the men were never actually arrested, for it was a blackmailer's paradise. There were few gay people in any major American city who had not crossed paths with these knights of morality.

The whole social milieu at the time created among homosexuals a deep-seated suspicion of everyone else. This constant state of suspicion and fear took a heavy psychological toll of gay men and women.

Sarah's son, Charles, had been gay all his life. He was one of the gay people who felt distressed by his homosexuality, but married a woman, had four children, and led a double life. It was only at the age of thirty-five that Charles separated from his wife and established a love relationship with another man. Charles and his lover maintained their relationship for ten years. Sarah accepted this arrangement and did nothing that would cause further problems for her son and his lover.

At the age of forty-six Charles moved into a small house with his lover. In those days men living together was a sure sign of homosexuality, and the retribution from the community was swift and severe. The lover was fired from his job, and Charles' job was threatened as well. Charles blamed himself for his lover's dismissal from his job. "Oh! what have I done to this man," he said to Sarah, as if he and not the prejudiced employer had harmed his lover.

Sarah was sitting at home when her daughter, with tears in her eyes, called her to the phone. The call was from the town were Charles lived. Charles and his lover had committed suicide. The two of them had sat in their car, closed the garage door, and started the engine. They were found in the back seat, cuddled together, their hands clasped.

It was discrimination that victimized these two men. It was prejudice that cared little about the character or the quality of their relationship. To have a lover of the same sex was enough cause for ostracism, and for Sarah's son and his lover, it happened once too often. With her son's death came Sarah's resolve to work toward the day when no other mother would have to see her child die needlessly, a day when no other mother would see friends refuse to come to the funeral service because a homosexual was being buried. When the first Gay Liberation Day parade was held in New York City in 1970, Sarah was the only parent to march. When Sarah took her batch of letters that day, she knew the problems the parents faced; she would answer their letters kindly and completely.

At two forty-five the Steering Committee finished its business and went downstairs to the meeting room.

There were thirty-eight people at the meeting, thirty-one of whom were parents. The rest were sons and daughters, gay and straight, who had come with them. Some of the parents had been attending these meetings for a long time, and Ann Browne saw them chatting amiably with other parents and children. The Winklers were a good example. They had been coming to the Sunday meetings for over a year. Their son Robert, aged twenty, was going to college out of town and living with his lover. A few minutes after the Winklers arrived, Robert and his lover walked into the room. He went over to his parents, kissed them, and sat down next to his father. His lover shook hands with the parents and sat down next to Robert's mother. They talked together until the meeting began.

"I think we should get started now," said Mrs. Manford. "I see there are quite a few new parents here today, and I want to be sure we have enough time for everyone to speak. But before we do anything else, Sarah wants to talk about the parade."

For the benefit of those in the group who were new, Sarah gave an account of the origin of the Gay Liberation Day Parade.

There was a gay bar in New York called The Stonewall. For many years its patrons had been accustomed to police harassment. On many occasions the police had raided the bar and lined up the patrons on the street, only to let them leave a few minutes later. This procedure was typical of police tactics in all the gay bars in New York, as well as around the country.

One night in 1969 the police raided the Stonewall. But that time the bar patrons resisted. When the police lined them up outside the bar, the men broke out in a chorus of anger. The years of humiliation, blackmail and discrimination were symbolized by the cold blue uniforms of the police. The men began to throw whatever objects were at hand. Bottles, glasses, even coins were hurled through the air at the officers, who were not used to such strong resistance from gay men. For the first time in New York City, or anywhere else in the country, the "sissies" protested.

The police were thrown completely off guard. In desperation, they ran for cover—into The Stonewall! At that point the situation had reversed itself completely. The gay men were hounding the police, who had taken refuge in the bar. Outside the gay men chanted and yelled, until police reinforcements arrived and the crowd eventually dispersed.

Out of that night of confrontation at The Stonewall came the slogan of the gay liberation movement: "Out of the closets and into the streets." Some of the bar's patrons vowed to begin organizations devoted to gaining gay people their civil rights and ending the years of discrimination.

Each year since 1969 gay people in New York City have commemorated the Stonewall raid with a parade in which thousands of gay people, some representing the many organizations now existing and others participating as individuals, march from Greenwich Village to Central Park. Passing the site where The Stonewall stood, they chant the slogan, "Out of the closets and into the streets." Each year, heeding the call, more and more people join the march, parading openly in the streets of the city.

The first Gay Liberation Day parade was an event of great importance in the movement. The idea soon spread to a number of other cities. Today more than a dozen cities celebrate the Stonewall raid with a parade, always during the last week in June.

The parade is extremely important to Parents of Gays, because it offers an opportunity for parents to support their children publicly. And of all the groups that march in the parade, none is more important than the Parents of Gays, nor is any other group more enthusiastically applauded as they pass by.

Sarah had marched the whole route last year. She wanted to do it again this year, but she knew the walk would be too long for her, as for many of the other parents. She proposed that Parents of Gays rent a flat-bed truck for the day so that those who wanted to could ride on it. When someone suggested they ride in a car, Sarah objected. "We shouldn't be enclosed in a car where we can't be seen."

The treasurer thought this an excellent moment to pass the hat for the monthly collection. At the same time, she circulated the sign-up sheet so that parents could write their names and addresses for the mailing list. "Make sure the pen comes back," called Edna, who was in charge of that. At that point she became very conscious of the new parents in the room. "New parents didn't come today to hear us talk about gallivanting around in a big truck," she suggested. "They have other things on their minds."

"How much good do you think all this demonstrating does?" The question came from a man who had come to a meeting for the first time. "The majority of people are against you. They don't approve of homosexuality, and they don't approve of homosexuals demonstrating. It's a fact of life. You don't have to like it, but it's a fact. I think you force people to be against you because the demonstration makes them uptight."

Rae Kameny, whose astronomer son had been fired from his government job some years ago, responded, "Look, if our children stay in the closet, people will be against them. If they come out and demand their rights, people will be against them. So it's their decision whether they want to stand up and be counted or not. We've decided to stand with them. It's true that it turns some people off, but it turns other people on."

"You talk about coming out of the closet," said the newcomer. "I don't see very many people who've come out. It's just the kids, the young ones. People with important jobs aren't coming out so much. How many people do you think have come out?"

One of the parents yelled, "Millions, at least twenty million!" She was angry at the truth of the man's comment. The public emergence of homosexuals has been a slow process, and it was initiated primarily by the younger generation. Older gays have been more conservative. They have more to lose. While this pattern is changing, it's still true that the gay liberation movement has been led by people in their twenties.

The man who had been speaking said that people don't understand homosexuality; that people get upset when they hear that someone they know or the child of someone they know is a homosexual. "When you tell these people, they don't know what to say and they get embarrassed. They don't want to know about it. I agree with them. They don't need to know. My son is gay. He can run his own life the way he wants. I can't do anything to stop him. But I can't see how advertising and flaunting this thing helps anyone. It just gets a lot of attention and then you have to start explaining things to people and answering to relatives. It can get very complicated."

That was all Mrs. Halleck had to hear. She had only one child, a boy, and he was gay. Mrs. Halleck was an old-timer at Parents of Gays, and she and her son were regulars at these meetings. "That's crap! You're not worried about other people getting embarrassed. You're worried about your own embarrassment. And what do you care if he flaunts it? It's his life, and if you believe he has the right to run his life, then what business is it of yours how he does it?" Then Mrs. Halleck became aware of how angry she had become and apologized for speaking so sharply. She continued more quietly. "With age I've become less tolerant. I mean less tolerant of people who hurt their own children. I'm talking about parents who come to Parents of Gays once and never come back again. I give them credit for coming the first time, and I think the ones who return are just marvelous. Even though they still have their problems, they're trying to

cope with them. But so many people come just once and
that's it. I'm angry at them. I'm angry because every time
they say something disapproving about what gays are
doing, they're putting their own kids down.

"How can you be against your own child? A child
doesn't ask to be born, so you should want the joys and
the tribulations of raising a kid in this world. And you
owe it to your children to teach them everything that will
help them to stand on their own two feet. And I want to
tell you this—every time you put down what our children
do to change society's attitudes, you push them farther
away from what they want and need: their civil rights.
The kids demonstrate for a good reason—they demonstrate for justice."

Nowhere else could parents be talked to this way
and expected to listen. No professional could say these
words, nor could a gay liberation leader. But in this
group parents listened to what other parents had to say.
All of them had raised their children with the usual
parental dreams of heterosexual happiness, and all had
had to rethink their attitudes and their feelings about
their children. No other group could make themselves
heard so well.

Ann Browne had been sitting quietly next to her
father, wanted him to say something. She knew her father
wouldn't begin, so she asked the questions she hoped he
wanted answered.

"How did you parents come to accept your gay
children?"

Rae Kameny answered Ann's question. "I cried a
lot. I went out and looked for all the books I could find
about homosexuality. It was twenty-five years ago, when
things were much worse, so I felt ashamed to talk to
anyone. And those books were the worst things I ever
saw. One psychiatrist wrote a book telling how all
homosexuals were unhappy people and never could be

happy. He said they were all destined to lead lonely lives, and their old age would be filled with depression. Then there was another book by a psychiatrist that said a boy becomes a homosexual because of his mother. Another wrote that the father causes it. Then there were books that said that homosexual men like to seduce little boys—that homosexual men force children to have sex with them. And all the time I was thinking about my son, who had just been fired by the federal government for being a homosexual, even though he did his job well.

"Do you know what those books did for me? They made me feel that my son was dying of some disease. And not only was he sick, he was a pervert, a child molester, a sinner. And he was going to lead a horribly lonely life. And who was to blame for all this? Me. I did this to him.

"Reading those books was plenty of cause for a mother to cry."

Ann was touched by Mrs. Kameny's words. "What happened to make you change your mind about your son?"

"I started to listen to him. Your best education is your own child. I wanted to know what kind of life he led. I especially wanted to find out what kind of friends he had. I know about people. I can judge what kind of character a person has. You don't need to be a psychiatrist to do that. So I met his friends, and I talked with them a lot. I made sure that Frank brought them over to my house whenever he could so they would feel comfortable with me.

"Do you know what I found? I found out they were nice people. They were all educated people like him, and they were good friends for him, the kind of friends I would have liked Frank to have no matter what he was. And Frank was the same son I had always known and loved. My son was nothing like what the psychiatrists said he was.

"When Frank got fired from his job he said that he didn't want anyone else to go through what he did. No one else should be fired from a job because of what they do in their private life. So he decided he was going to join the battle to have homosexuality included under our civil rights laws. And he did that before the Stonewall riots, and before the gay liberation movement started a few years ago. He did that when homosexuals were still being beaten up on the streets by the cops and everyone else. It wasn't very fashionable to be a homosexual then, like it is for some people today. It was hard—very hard.

"And I felt proud of what he was doing. He stood up and spoke his mind and forced people to listen to him. Sometimes he got hurt for it. He didn't work very much—no one would give him a job. But he never stopped.

"He was just appointed Commissioner for Human Rights in Washington, D.C. Now everyone knows the work of Frank Kameny, one of the earliest pioneers in fighting discrimination against gays. He won his fight. The courts in Washington, D.C., said that no one can be fired from a job because of their sexual preference. Now you tell me: Should I feel sad or proud of my son? Should I have listened to those terrible books that only wanted me to feel guilty because I had done something awful to him? Or should I have listened to him, and supported him in what he wanted to do? I chose my son, and thank God I did. If I had listened to the psychiatrists I would have hurt him. By listening to him I helped him—and I helped myself. I'm proud of my son."

"But what made the change in you?" Ann pleaded.

"I stopped thinking of myself. I stopped saying, 'Why did this have to happen to me?' I stopped thinking about what it meant to me, and my shame, and the problems it presented for me. Oh, I know what parents think. I thought the same things. How am I going to tell my family about this? What will the neighbors say?

What will people think of me when I walk down the street? I was upset by the idea that people in the neighborhood would think to themselves, 'Poor Mrs. Kameny. She has this terrible trouble. She must feel so bad.' Ugh! And I was upset because I wouldn't have any grandchildren. A lot of gays get married, but I knew that Frank wouldn't—and that meant I would never become a grandmother. My husband was dead, so grandchildren would have filled up my time a little more.

"I don't know just when things started to change. I think it was one night when some of Frank's friends were over at the house. One of them had just had a very bad scene with his parents. The boy was entrapped by the police in a public toilet. The officer was standing by a urinal masturbating when Frank's friend came in. The officer asked Frank's friend to touch him, and when he did, the officer flashed a badge and arrested the boy for homosexual behavior.

"The boy's parents went into a panic. They hadn't known he was gay. They screamed at him about what a terrible thing this was for the family, the shame they would suffer in the neighborhood because of this perverted thing he did. And the boy was terrified. He was terrified about being arrested, terrified about a public trial and the possibility of being fired from his job because of it. He was terrified about the possibility of going to jail, where homosexuals are regularly raped by other prisoners with the consent of the prison guards, who occasionally do some raping themselves. And worst of all, he was terrified of his own family. Frank was the only person he could turn to.

"While Frank was talking to this boy and trying to calm him down, I thought about the boy's family and how they were treating him. Why didn't they stand up and get angry at the behavior of the police? Why didn't they accuse the officer who spent all night in a toilet,

trying to entice everybody who walked in? Why should
this officer have the right to arrest anyone for immoral
behavior? You tell me whose behavior was immoral. I
was angry at the parents for not thinking about these
things. They weren't thinking of their son, they were
only thinking about themselves.

"Then I started to wonder about my own reactions. I started to consider whether I was being as selfish
as this boy's parents. And I think I was. I'd thought about
what my son's homosexuality meant to me and how it
affected me—not about his life and what it meant to him
and his friends. It was a turning point for me. What was
important were his goals in life, not what I wanted for
him. He chose his profession and he chose his life-style.
If I'm for him, I have to respect both. He doesn't have to
make my life complete. I have to do that myself. When
you get to a certain age you have to realize that your
children are grown up and they have a right to choose—
and their choice can't be based on how their parents feel
about things. If you love your child you have to say, 'The
hell with the world. I don't love the world, or the
neighbors. I love my son.'"

Ann Browne wished her father would say something. It seemed to her that Mrs. Kameny would know
what to say to him. But Mr. Browne sat still, his eyes still
red. Ann felt she had to speak again.

"How do you get to the feelings inside yourself?
I'm asking about my sister, who's living in California
now. My parents are in turmoil. They keep hoping that
she'll change, that she'll become heterosexual again. She
used to be married, but she left her husband and went to
live with another woman. My mother wouldn't come
here today. She hasn't accepted this thing at all. I think my
parents are split on how to handle the situation, and
that's making things even worse."

All eyes in the room centered on the elderly man

sitting next to Ann Browne. He was obviously her father. When he didn't take the opportunity to say anything, one of the other parents spoke to him.

"Are you the father?"

Mr. Browne nodded his head in assent.

"How do you feel about your daughter?"

Mr. Browne obviously didn't want to answer. "It's a bad time for me to talk. I just want to listen to what you have to say." Ann Browne was distressed to hear her father say this, as were the rest of the parents. But his distress was so noticeable that they did not intrude upon his privacy, though many of them wished they had a chance to help alleviate the pain he showed so plainly.

There was a brief silence at this point. Many of the other parents wondered whether this was the right time to ask the questions that were on their minds. Irving Polansky was the first to speak.

"My son, who's twenty-three, wants to tell his grandparents, my parents, about his homosexuality. Warren has been 'out' for quite a while, and my wife and I were the first he ever told. He feels very good about his homosexuality. He's never had any problems with it, and he gets along very well with his lover. They live together. Now he says that he would like to tell my parents. I'm not so sure about that. Why do they need to know? Both of them are in their seventies. They come from a different generation. I just don't think they'll understand as my wife and I do. They're still very religious people. They came here as immigrants, and they still have a lot of the old ways about them."

Mr. Jones, the man who had questioned whether homosexuals should "flaunt" themselves in demonstrations, instantly saw the inconsistency in Mr. Polansky's statement. "Look, a little while ago you guys were pushing the idea that homosexuals should come out of the closet. They should stand up and be seen and fight for their rights. Now you say that's okay as long as your son doesn't do it in your family. Go ahead and shake up strangers but don't shake up my parents."

"But they wouldn't understand," Mr. Polansky interrupted.

"According to that kind of thinking your son wouldn't have told you. You're from a different generation, too. What makes you so much smarter than your parents? They're not immigrants any more."

The logic of this statement exposed the weakness of Polansky's position. In truth, Polansky didn't entirely disagree with coming out. He was in conflict about it, and his conflict reflected his feelings about his own relationship to his parents, a conflict that his son, Warren, did not share. Mr. Jones also felt a bit smug about his clear-sighted comment. For a while he had felt that some of the other parents were lecturing him for being disloyal to his son, pretending that they had all the answers. It was reassuring to find that even some of the old-timers at Parents of Gays still had problems they hadn't worked out.

"Mr. Jones, you haven't told us how you feel about homosexuality," one of the other parents said.

Jones's answer was to the point and truthful. "I'm a religious man and I come from a religious family. And that's how I've raised my children. The purpose of sex is to conceive children. Any other kind of sex is a sin. That's my religious upbringing and that's what I believe."

"Do you believe that you or your wife is responsible for your son's becoming a homosexual?"

"No, he's responsible. I believe people have free will and choose their own lives. That's what he's chosen for himself, and I believe it's an immoral choice. I'm not happy with it and neither is my wife."

For the next half-hour the discussion centered on religion. The argument got very heated at times, particularly when the gays in the group joined in. Gay people have been called sinners for so long that those in the group were very sensitive to Mr. Jones's remarks. The gays had an answer to every argument in the Bible against homosexuality. The story of Sodom and Gomorrah had to do with God's anger at the violation of the code of hospitality, not at homosexuality (a specious argument). The sin of Onan was coitus interruptus, not masturbation (correct), so it has nothing to do with homosexuality (incorrect).

The discussion got nowhere. Two opposing positions were being advocated. On the one hand some parents believed that homosexuality is a sin, and gays on the other hand said that it isn't. In the heat of the argument everyone forgot about Mr. Jones, and they lost sight of his problem—the conflict between his love for his son and his belief in his religion.

Mr. Jones's predicament is common. People with strong religious beliefs sometimes feel they are in the position of having to choose between their child and their faith. Sometimes this is true, but only because they insist that one give in completely to the other. For these parents either the child will win and the parent will lose his religion, or the religion will win and they will lose the child. With this kind of reasoning, the parent must always lose something. Reconciling the two may or may not be possible. It becomes the responsibility of the parent to try.

Mr. Jones would have been helped more if the others had recognized his conflicting feelings instead of trying to proselytize for homosexuality. As it was, Mr. Jones had every reason to feel that many of the people there looked down on the religious beliefs that had served him so well all his life. They would have been more helpful if they had thought how difficult it must have been for him to come to the meeting that day and expose his bias against homosexuality. It was a sense of honesty and strong character that brought Mr. Jones to the meeting, and this was overlooked by his opponents. Mr. Jones touched a defensive chord in some of the other parents, and particularly in the gays. So they attacked his religious beliefs instead of asking themselves why they were so defensive.

There were other kinds of defensiveness at the meeting. So heavily charged a topic as homosexuality in the family is found to elicit strong reactions. The issue that made the gays most defensive was the question of causation. When parents would ask where homosexuality came from, what caused it, the answer was usually quick and automatic. "It's caused by the same thing that causes heterosexuality" was one of the more common responses. Or someone would ask, "How come you never ask why your 'straight' [heterosexual] children turned out that way?" Why were the gays so defensive about a question that almost all parents ask?

Most gays are very sensitive to questions about causation. What they fear is that the questioner really means, "What causes homosexuality, and how can it be changed?" They interpret the question as the first step in an attempt to try to make them heterosexual. Their anger is a response to this supposed intention. In fact, most people who ask the question do have it in mind to also try to change the gay person's sexual preference, so the reaction of gays is not entirely unreasonable. It's just that they jump the gun.

The gays' defensiveness was challenged by one of the parents, to whom the meeting had been very exciting. He suggested that it was an indication of their insecurity about themselves. "My daughter is a lesbian, and she has always told me that she's never been as happy as she is today. I believed her, but listening to some of you, I'm not so sure now."

Unfortunately the gays at the meeting reacted to these cogent remarks with more defensiveness. They were young, and some of them were active in the gay liberation movement, where they had to defend themselves all the time. It was only when Mrs. Kameny spoke up that good sense prevailed.

"Let me say something. What you've said is true. Gays are very insecure about some things people say, and sometimes they jump too quick. They still have a lot to learn about themselves. That's why we invite them to come to our meetings, so that they can learn about themselves, just as the parents have to learn about themselves. But don't be too hard on them for that. It's the price people pay for being discriminated against for so long. You want to know whether gays are happy. Right now homosexuals aren't as happy as they have a right to be. It's not a matter of whether they're happy. It's whether they have a right to live a happy life. Some of us are here to try to change society so that our children can be as happy as they have a right to be."

Jeannie Manford noticed that the meeting had already gone beyond its scheduled time. She invited all the parents to return the next month, and the meeting was adjourned.

SOME *DOS* AND *DON'TS* FOR PARENTS OF GAYS

1. *Don't* rush the process of trying to understand your child's homosexuality.

   Do take the time to seek information about the lives of gay people from other parents of gays, friends of your gay child, literature and, most of all, from your own son or daughter.

2. *Don't* criticize your son or daughter for being different.

   Do listen to what your son or daughter's life is like, and what kind of experiences he or she has had in the world.

3. *Don't* blame your own feelings on your child.

   Do accept that you are responsible for your negative reactions.

4. *Don't* expect your children to make up for your own failures in life.

   Do help your child to set his or her individual goals, even though these may differ drastically from your own.

5. *Don't* try to force your child to conform to your ideas of proper sexual behavior.

   Do try to develop trust and openness by allowing your child to choose his or her own lifestyle.

6. *Don't* blame yourself that your son or daughter is gay.

   Do be proud of your child's capacity for having loving relationships.

7. *Don't* respond to anger with anger.

   Do look for the injured feelings underneath the anger and respond to them.

8. *Don't* discriminate against your own child.

Do defend him or her against discrimination.

9. *Don't* demand that your son or daughter live up to your idea of what a man or woman should be.

   Do allow your child to develop his or her own personality.

10. *Don't* try to break up love relationships.

    Do respect your child's right to find out how to choose the right person to love and how to make relationships last.

11. *Don't* insist that your morality is the only right one.

    Do say, "I love you."

12. *Don't* assume that your child should see a professional psychotherapist.

    Do get professional help for anyone in the family, including yourself, who becomes severely depressed over your child's homosexuality.

Society,
Medicine
and
Homosexuality

So far, this book has discussed the experiences of a number of families and their gay children. We have seen how different families used the homosexuality of a son or daughter to create either greater family unity or greater family dissension.

The following section has a different function. Here we will examine two important and pervasive misconceptions that affect the lives of gay people. These are: our rigid ideas of masculinity and femininity, and the idea that homosexuality is a mental illness.

Gay people have suffered a great deal from discrimination because they violate society's standards of masculine and feminine behavior. They have also been victims of misguided theories of physicians and psychiatrists.

We have not attempted to give a complete account of the origins of "homophobia"—the fear and hatred of gay people. A longer and more technical book would be required to examine that subject in detail, but we hope enough is presented here to give parents a better understanding of gay people's distrust of the medical profession. If you're interested in learning more about the origins of discrimination against gay people, I urge you to refer to the books listed in the bibliography.

chapter eleven

HENRY BURKE'S CURE

I was introduced to Henry Burke at a party. It was a festive occasion, and the last thing I expected was a consultation. Burke was a man in his middle fifties, gray at the temples, tall and slender. When he learned that I was a psychologist who specialized in sexuality, his expression changed and he looked at me more intently.

"Have you ever heard of testosterone?" said Burke.

I nodded my head.

"My doctor has been giving me injections of testosterone for the past two years. It isn't helping. Do you have any suggestions?"

I hoped that Mr. Burke could not see how horrified I was to hear that he had been receiving testosterone injections for two years. It was too long a period of time. I knew that he was trying to tell me something about himself. Since a party was not the place to discuss serious psychological and medical questions, I suggested that he see me privately in my office the next week.

A few days later he arrived at my office and told me his problem.

Mr. Burke had been married for twenty-seven years and had three children, two boys and a girl. All of his children were now married, and he and his wife lived quietly at home. Mr. Burke was gay. He had always been gay. Throughout his married life Henry Burke had maintained a clandestine sexual life unknown to his wife. His homosexual activities had begun long before he met her, and they had continued into the present.

Burke's homosexual life consisted entirely of quickly consummated genital contacts. Driven by the need for sexual release, he sought out other men, regardless of the risk involved. Like other men who live in this precarious way, he found opportunities for anonymous sex in the big city. He went to the places frequented by other men who wanted sex without intimacy or self-disclosure.

Haunted by the fear of exposure and consequent scandal, Henry Burke and the multitude of men like him were forced to seek sexual gratification in a carefully controlled environment of anonymity and impersonality. Sexual acts were performed in silence with strangers who would always remain strangers. After orgasm the men would separate, saying little or nothing to each other, and knowing that neither of them could afford to be friendly. They would dress, and leave as quietly as they came together, until their needs reasserted themselves and the process would be repeated with another man at another time.

For Burke it was a painful life. Each time as he dressed after one of these quick, cold encounters he felt as if his mind and body were pitted against each other, as if his genitals were driving him to actions that brought temporary relief but permanent psychological pain. The lies he told his wife, his fear of contracting V.D. and transmitting it to her, his anxiety lest his homosexuality contaminate his children in some bizarre and unforeseen way preyed on his mind continually.

Trapped and tortured, he found escape in his fantasies. Each time he came home after one of his sexual encounters, Henry would console himself by dreaming a special dream.

He was in a large dark room. It was a private and secluded place, far from the world and all the pressures of his daily life. The darkness of the room reassured him. He walked about slowly, waiting for his eyes to adjust to the lack of light.

After a few minutes he was able to make out the shadowy outlines of other men who had silently entered the room. A hand reached out and touched Henry's arm. He stopped for a moment, turning hesitantly in the direction of the shadowy figure. Then the hand began to caress him, gently at first, touching only the uppermost parts of his arm, then in longer strokes from his elbow to his fingers. Henry began to stroke the man who had been stroking him. They moved closer to one another and embraced.

Ten minutes later both men had experienced their orgasms. Henry was preparing to leave and travel home to his family, when suddenly a door was thrown open and light flooded the room. Henry found himself face to face with his companion in the bright light. To Henry's surprise, the man was smiling, smiling at Henry, and his eyes radiated warmth and caring. Henry melted under his gaze, and moved toward him. The man said, "Hello."

Henry always awoke from his dream at this point. He never allowed it to continue because it caused him too much pain. He knew that it was bringing him in touch with his need for a close emotional relationship with a man. He had denied this need for many years, but he could never suppress it entirely. The dream came too close to what he wanted for himself. It was too dangerous a threat to the reality of his wife and family, for whose sake he had tamed these feelings by confining himself to quick encounters in depersonalized circumstances.

Whatever he did, Henry Burke was doomed to

feelings of depression. On the one hand, he felt guilty about lying to his wife and family, manufacturing business engagements that didn't exist and counterfeiting sexual interest in his wife. On the other, he was consumed with anger at being cheated of happiness and being forced to deny his sexual and emotional need for another man. He had neither a marriage nor a lover, and he felt incapable of making a success of either kind of partnership.

Furthermore, Henry Burke, at the age of fifty-five, was still struggling with a number of unresolved conflicts about his mother. His mother had always wanted a girl and she had been severely disappointed by the birth of a son, who the doctors told her would be her only child. She never let the boy forget her disappointment and when he was very young she began to dress him and treat him as a girl. For the six or seven years of his life, Henry did not rebel against his mother's attempt to feminize him, though his father sporadically interfered.

Henry Burke believed that his homosexuality had been caused by these attitudes of his mother's. To him, his difficulties with his marriage and his discomfort relating to his children were all part of the same problem: a profound confusion about his sexual identity. Like many people in our society, Henry believed that homosexuality could be produced by confusing a child about his or her sexual identity—that is to say, by creating a conflict between a child's biological sex and his social role as "boy" or "girl."

Two years ago something unexpected happened. Henry's younger son Roger had come home suddenly to talk to his parents. Roger's wife wasn't with him. Henry knew that there were problems in their marriage, but he wasn't certain what these were. Roger told them that night. He said that he and his wife were getting divorced. He told his parents that he was gay, and that he was leaving his wife for a male lover. He told them about his personal struggle with his homosexuality, how hard he had tried to deny it, and how he had even married in an attempt to "cure" it. But, though his wife had been understanding and supportive, he had decided that his marriage was a sham. Then he met a young man and fell in love with him. He could no longer continue living with his wife, making a pretense of heterosexuality. They had agreed to part.

Roger wasn't asking his parents for permission to get divorced, but he felt they had a right to know why his marriage was breaking up and what direction he was taking. He wasn't sure whether he would remain with his current lover; he didn't really know whether he wanted to live with anyone at this period in his life. He knew that he needed time to examine his feelings, and construct a new life for himself. He was going to take the opportunity to think about things, but he wasn't going to deny his needs in the meantime, or worry about what other people would think. Roger closed the conversation as quickly as he had opened it. He made it clear that he didn't want to talk any further at that time. Having accomplished what he set out to do, Roger said goodbye to his parents and left them alone to discuss the unexpected news.

Henry and Elizabeth Burke were both frozen in disbelief. Neither of them had ever had the slightest inkling that Roger was sexually interested in men. He was an athlete, a keen and successful competitor in any sport he chose to play. He had been very popular with the girls since he was a kid. Finding out that his son was gay took Henry completely by surprise.

Henry's first reaction was a splitting headache that lasted for three days. He could feel the muscles of his body binding him like a straitjacket. His head seemed to sink into his chest and his shoulders were weighted down by the steadily increasing pressure of a terrible new fear. He would find his hands clenched so tightly that they ached from the physical strain. On the third day, with a great effort, Henry forced himself to look at a picture of his son. Just then, the feeling of physical tension was suddenly released, and a wave of guilt swept over him, taking its place.

To Henry Burke, a man with pressing unresolved conflicts about homosexuality, the realization that his son was also a homosexual seemed to destroy what faith he had in himself as a father. He was now double damned. Just as he blamed his mother for his own homosexual desires, he now blamed himself for causing his son's homosexuality. Things seemed perfectly clear to Henry. In some unfathomable way his younger son had inherited his homosexuality, and the boy's disastrous marriage was actually Henry's fault. Henry Burke abused himself psychologically by perceiving every problem Roger faced in life as evidence of defective genes transmitted by the father to the son. It made no difference to Henry that he had invented two different causes of homosexuality: in his own case, being dressed as a girl, and in his son's, a bad genetic inheritance. His eagerness to blame himself for this son's homosexuality, because of his own guilt about being gay, was much more powerful than logic.

In the course of the next week Henry's self-inflicted mental anguish got worse and worse. His thinking began to clear a little after the initial shock wore off and Henry started to realize how many conflicting feelings this crisis had brought to the surface. He was struck by the parallels between himself and his son. Both had recognized but denied their homosexuality for many years. Both had married in order to prove their masculinity and cure themselves of their homosexual desires. Both had kept their homosexuality hidden from their wives. Both had lied to cover up absences from home, resented the necessity of doing so, and felt remorse after such deception. Both of them had been so frightened by the possibility of public exposure that they had shared their secret with no one. Least of all did father and son share their common predicament with one another. Each felt alone, unlovable and unloved.

But Henry realized that the parallels ended there. There was one highly significant difference between him and his son. Roger was doing something about the situation. He was trying to make a new life for himself. Roger was not going to remain in a marriage that was as unfair to his wife as it was to him. He was prepared to come out to his parents and other members of his family. He had redirected all the energy once employed in concealing his homosexuality and was using it to make a future for himself. Henry didn't know whether Roger would make a better job of it the second time around, but at least he had a chance to try.

That's what got to Henry. His son had found hope. This was something that Henry still felt incapable of doing. Henry saw his son doing all the things he wished he could do if only he had the nerve. Henry's marriage was no better than Roger's, and Henry's wife, Elizabeth, had for many years been as unhappy as Henry and even more confused. She blamed herself for the distance between herself and her husband. Henry knew it might actually be a relief for Elizabeth to find out that she was not responsible for the failure of their marriage, but he couldn't bring himself to talk to her about it.

Henry looked at the giant step his son had taken. He admired the boy's honesty, his willingness to suffer the problems of learning a new life-style, and his courage in facing the possible consequences of his actions in a prejudiced community. But Henry also hated Roger for doing these things. He was embarrassed. He felt humiliated. As he saw it, not only had he caused his son's homosexuality, but he was doubly a failure as a man for not being able to face his own feelings and take the honest steps that his son had taken. He was jealous of Roger. He was envious of Roger's finding a man to love. No matter how hard he tried to suppress these feelings, they constantly haunted him.

He was beset with conflicting feelings of love and hate for his son. Love and hate are both strong masters. First one, then the other would gain the upper hand in Henry's mind. If Henry wanted to encourage Roger in his new life, his jealousy stopped him. If he wanted to say something hostile to his son, his love prevented it. Henry could neither express his love for his son nor see himself as worthy of anyone's love, particularly his son's. He could never allow himself to hurt the boy, but he could and did turn his envy of his son into hatred of himself.

Henry Burke put himself on trial. Was Henry Burke a man? No, he was a homosexual. Guilty. Was Henry Burke a moral man? No, he was a sinner and a sodomite. Guilty. Was Henry Burke a good husband to his wife? No, he did not love her, nor was he interested in satisfying her. Guilty. Was Henry Burke a good father? No, he had caused his son's homosexuality. Guilty. Besides, he was resentful of his son's freedom of action. Guilty again. Not a man; not a husband; not a father.

Henry Burke awoke one day in the hospital. His suicide attempt had failed. He had gone into the garage, closed the doors, started the car, and waited to die. Perhaps he didn't really want to die, since he'd left his briefcase in the house where his wife was sure to find it. When she did, she ran to the garage and found him unconscious. He continued to lie to his wife, inventing all sorts of reasons for the suicide attempt, but he now knew he had to talk to someone and get some relief from his emotional turmoil. He would have liked to follow in his son's footsteps, but he convinced himself that he was too old. He would try to wipe out his homosexual desires. For the first time in his life, he sought professional help.

The psychiatrist was a man of standing in the community, with a reputation for working with homosexual men and making them heterosexual. Henry told him the long story of his unhappy marriage, his lonely sexual encounters, and the effect of his son's coming out, all of which had culminated in his attempted suicide. He wanted relief from his feelings of worthlessness, and he wanted to rid himself of his homosexual desires and substitute "good" heterosexual feelings.

The psychiatrist offered Henry Burke relief. He promised to cure him. In addition to psychotherapy twice a week, the doctor informed him that there were drugs that could help him with his problem. Henry would no longer have to worry about wanting other men, the doctor said. After treatment his marriage would be more successful than in the past. He would not have to lead a homosexual life like his son. Henry got his first injection of testosterone, and continued to receive it every week for the next two years.

Psychotherapy was useful in some ways. Henry was able at last to discuss the feelings he had been concealing from everyone; but therapy made no change in his sexual desires. Neither did the testosterone. Though the physician had said the testosterone would decrease his homosexual inclinations, it seemed to have no effect upon him whatsoever. He was at a loss to know what else to do, and like many desperate people, he kept telling himself that perhaps in time the treatment would work. After two years he was convinced of its uselessness. Now he wanted to know if there was a more effective means of curing homosexuality.

Henry Burke finished his story. Although I was very interested in finding out more about his unusual experience, my first concern was to direct him to a physician who could acquaint him with the dangers of the "treatment" he was receiving. I referred him to a colleague who was thoroughly familiar with endocrine functions. Burke was about to find out that his testosterone injections might have done serious damage to his body.

Testosterone is a hormone produced in the testes. It's considered the "male sex hormone," and in adolescence it controls the development of the male secondary sex characteristics such as pubic hair, the growth of the genitals, the voice change, and the production of sperm. Testosterone also seems to affect sexual interest and desire. Without it, men (and women too) would feel very little, if any, sexual desire.

Normally functioning testes produce testosterone in sufficient quantities throughout most of a man's life. There are very few situations in which the injection of artificially produced testosterone is necessary. Even when the use of testosterone is medically appropriate, injections over as long a period as two years can result in physical damage.

A man's body requires only a limited amount of testosterone. When a man with normal testes receives injections of testosterone his testes may stop producing their own supply. Over a short period of time this need not cause alarm, since the testes will return to normal functioning when treatment is terminated. But over a long period—and two years is long—the disuse of the testes can result in atrophy. They shrivel up and the cells can be damaged. With sufficient disuse the injury can be permanent and the testes may be unable to resume production of testosterone. The cells that produce sperm can also be damaged. Yet these are not the worst possible dangers from the *overuse* of the drug.

One of the most prevalent types of cancer in men

is cancer of the prostate gland, an organ lying just below the bladder. Every good physical examination includes the prostate. Since the gland is close to the lower part of the rectum, the physician can feel it by inserting his finger. This makes some men feel uncomfortable, but it is one of the most important parts of an examination.

The overuse of testosterone can aggravate incipient cancer of the prostate. While there is some disagreement as to whether prostatic cancer can be *caused* by the overuse of testosterone, such use unquestionably increases the probability of cancer occurring. Henry Burke's cure could result in cancer.

In this case the physician took a man with a normally functioning body and risked creating a serious physical problem for the sake of curing psychological problems. This physician may have caused atrophy of the testes, sterility, and increased chances that Burke would get cancer of the prostate. In other words, the physician's treatment was more destructive than the patient's complaint.

There have always been patients who died of the treatment and not the disease. Errors of diagnosis and subsequent errors of treatment, such as overuse of a drug, use of the wrong drug, or causing damage to one organ of the body while curing another, are typical ways medicine can cause harm instead of healing. Medical authorities have long been aware of this problem, and good medicine considers not only the availability of a cure, but whether or not the cure is preferable to the illness. There is even a special name for illness or distress caused by medical treatment: "iatrogenic disorder." This difficult word is a combination of two Greek words: *iatros*, meaning "physician," and *genesis*, meaning "origin." Therefore, iatrogenic disorders are those caused by physicians or medicine. I will have more to say about this concept in the next few chapters.

Henry Burke phoned me again two years later. I had heard nothing about him during the interim, and when he called I was interested to find out what had happened to him in the intervening time. I found him just as interested in talking to me about it. He came to see me.

My medical colleague had insisted that Burke immediately stop taking the testosterone so that he could ascertain whether any damage had been done by the heavy and prolonged chemical treatment. It was Burke's good fortune that no permanent injury was found. But Dr. Bory, the physician, gave Burke one heck of a bawling out for not seeking a consultation sooner. Dr. Bory was very angry that a man should go to such lengths to change his sexual preference, and he told Burke so. Burke was shocked, for the physician was a heterosexual man who shared none of Burke's negative feelings about homosexuality. Dr. Bory was blunt but effective in his approach.

"Look, Burke, you're fifty-five years old. You have a rotten marriage, which is making your life miserable, and it probably makes your wife miserable too. You have three kids, all of whom sound like they're pretty happy. You even have a son who's showing you how to improve your own life.

"Now you can do one of two things. You can go out and kill yourself, or you can make a new life for yourself. You're not too old, and you're entitled to some happiness. You live in a city where there are lots of opportunities to meet some very fine gay people, and maybe you can even learn to love another man.

"If you want to kill yourself, I can't help you. If you want me to refer you to a psychologist who will help you resolve your guilty feelings about being gay, then I'll do that. Now, which one will it be?"

Burke had never heard a physician talk like that

He had never met a heterosexual man with such positive views about homosexuality. He chose therapy.

Burke was referred to a psychologist who was himself gay. In the very first session the psychologist must have realized how important it was for Henry to know this, because he told him of his own sexual preference. At first Henry was taken aback by the revelation. His immediate impulse was to find a "normal" (heterosexual) therapist, but he decided to stick it out for a two-month period and then evaluate.

In those two months all of Henry's negative feelings about homosexuality were exposed. They became the basis for a new appraisal of his life. Henry was to remain with this therapist for two years, and to make a number of important changes.

The first change was Henry's willingness to talk to his son Roger about their homosexuality. To his surprise, Roger had already figured out that his father was gay and in the closet. He had sensed his father's discomfort, and although he had never broached the subject with him, he had wanted to. Roger told his father about his own experiences in the gay world. In an interesting reversal of roles, Roger volunteered to teach his father how to start making a new life for himself. Henry Burke was embarrassed that he needed his son's help, but he accepted it gratefully.

Then Burke came out to his wife. At first she felt hurt by the news. Then she got angry. For years she had blamed herself for her poor marriage, when all along things had been going on behind her back. She felt cheated of the opportunity to find a man who would give her the love and support she wanted in her life. She was angry because it had taken twenty-seven years of marriage before she learned the truth. She demanded a divorce, and Henry did not contest it. He was sorry that this had happened, but he knew that it was better for both of them. At least now she could make a new life for herself as well.

Henry Burke then came out to his other children. They were totally confused. First a brother turned out gay, then their father. Henry calmed them and said that he still loved them and hoped that their feelings toward him wouldn't change. They didn't, although the children are still just as confused as ever.

Burke stopped looking for "quickie" anonymous sex. He began to associate with other gay men and found that friendship and sex can be combined. He began to establish relationships with other men and even joined a local gay group, although he found most of the members were rather young and seemed uninterested in the things that interested him. This ever-widening circle of friends and acquaintances helped Henry find the kinds of people who satisfied his sexual and emotional needs.

He met a man who became very special to him. Jonathan is just about the same age as Henry and has also been married. They shared some experiences and problems, and this helped bring them together. They are now lovers and share an apartment. They are facing some problems in doing this after so many years of heterosexual marriage, but they persist, knowing that they have to establish a new style that will permit their love to grow. They work very hard at it.

Somewhere along the way—Henry wasn't sure when—he started to rethink his assumptions about the origin of his homosexuality. He had always believed that he was gay because his mother dressed him like a girl when he was young. He now recognized that his anger toward his mother was only a veil that hid his feelings of guilt. It was just another way of saying that he was abnormal. He still felt angry that his mother had mistreated him by making him feel unwanted, but he was no longer clinging tenaciously to the idea that she caused his homosexuality. Now that he was learning to feel good about himself he didn't need that excuse any more.

Burke's life had changed a great deal since I had seen him last. He was in the process of discovering himself to be, not just a gay person, but also a human being capable of finding happiness. I congratulated him on the changes and wished him the best in the future.

At one time the story of Henry Burke would have been a remarkable tale. It would have been an exception to the typical pattern of homosexual helplessness. Fortunately, times have changed, and more and more gay people are following the same path to self-expression and honesty. In most cases their experiences are positive. There are some, however, who still encounter severe discrimination, and who suffer because of it. But I have yet to hear of a single person who has regretted coming out and trying to find happiness. The rewards always seem to outweigh any negative consequences.

Henry Burke's whole experience in life and the treatment he received raise a host of questions. For instance, Burke blamed his homosexuality on his mother's desire to have a girl. Was he right? Can homosexuality be created that way? Burke also blamed himself for Roger's sexual preference. Is homosexuality inherited?

We might wonder why Burke condemned his own sexual preference so strongly. Where did he get his ideas of masculinity? What made him think of himself as a sinful, perverted man? Where do such attitudes come from?

Why did Burke choose to confide in a physician when he might have gone to a clergyman, a friend, his son, or any number of other people, including other gay people? Why did he think, as so many people do, that homosexuality is a medical problem? Is homosexuality an illness, either physical or psychological? If so, is there a successful medical or psychological treatment for it?

You may be aware that these questions are being argued by most professionals today. What is the current thinking of the scientific community about homosexuality, and what would these professionals think of Henry Burke's cure?

Parents are often caught between authorities who claim that homosexuality is a medical issue, and gays who reject medical or psychological help as unwarranted. It has become all the more confusing for parents as more and more professionals join gay people in renouncing the old medical notion of homosexuality as illness.

Our current attitudes are the result of thousands of years of civilization. Our conception of the family, our standards of morality, our style of sexuality, and our system of law were all developed in the past. By examining these value systems we can learn how our present-day attitudes toward sex were formed and what purpose they serve.

chapter twelve

MASCULINITY
AND HOMOSEXUALITY

It is not enough for someone to be born a male. In our society, training in boyhood is preparation for adult "masculinity." Being a "man" is very important, and not all the rewards of wealth or power can alleviate the suffering of one who feels himself a failure as a man. External successes help a bit, but not very much. More important is the internal feeling that you have conformed to the standard of masculine behavior demanded by your peers.

To most people, a masculine image is one of strength, both physical and emotional. A real man is competitive, aggressive and physically rough. He seeks dominance over other men in his competitive ventures, and always over women. But a homosexual evokes a different picture. The homosexual is emotionally weak and incapable of maintaining strength through adversity. Preferring quiet and cultural activity to competitive sports, the homosexual is a weakling, as fearful of physical harm as he is physically weak, and highly undependable in an emergency. A man is someone who pushes people around; the homosexual is the one who gets pushed.

In our society gays are considered as being somewhere between men and women, biologically one sex, but behaviorally the other. It is remarkable how often the heterosexual world perceives gay men as if they were women and lesbians as if they were men. This is, in large part, why many heterosexual people feel uncomfortable in the presence of a gay person. They are upset because the gay violates the rules of masculinity and femininity.

The idea of the gay person as a "flawed" man or woman is false, and it has always been false. Sociologists call this kind of distorted picture of a minority group a *stereotype*. We have lots of stereotypes in our society: Jews are called clannish and miserly; blacks are intellectually dull but happy; women are passive and emotional—ah yes! like homosexuals. A stereotype is a picture drawn by a majority that distorts the characteristics of a minority to justify exploitation and discrimination. Most of us belong to one minority group or another and can easily identify all the foolish ideas held by people who are not in that group.

The caricature of the homosexual is a vivid, dramatic picture that has been retouched periodically by western society in the course of thousands of years—and all of us have this picture imprinted upon our minds. Homosexuals have reacted to the stereotype in different ways. Some have accepted it and conformed to it, while others have rejected it. Both of these reactions can provide some understanding of its meaning and purpose.

I would like to emphasize that the stereotype of the homosexual is not simply true or false. We need to understand what purpose it serves. This may teach us how our own hopes and fears affect our perceptions of the lives of other people.

The homosexual stereotype was created by the heterosexual world. It is a picture intended to teach a moral or social rule, a summary of the majority's attitude toward a group of outcast rule-breakers. The picture expresses our contempt and anger at people who violate socially approved ways of behaving.

The stereotype serves two functions. First, it punishes a deviant group for disobeying the rules. In the most unflattering way, it describes the gay person as little more than the brittle shell of a man or a woman. Described mockingly as either a sissy or an amazon, the homosexual of the stereotype is not a person who should be taken too seriously.

However, punishing the homosexual is not the stereotype's most important function. *Its major function is to control the behavior of the heterosexual majority.* The stereotype is primarily a statement of how an incompetent man or woman behaves. It is a negative role model for others, a model that shows them that they will be punished if they act in the wrong way. It is in direct contrast with the positive role model that a society presents to its members. Let's explain this more carefully.

Our society, like any other, needs to teach a child, particularly a boy, how he should act so that he will grow up to be a "man." The boy is presented with two kinds of models (by "model" I mean an example of a man that the boy can copy). The first is the *positive role model,* someone who is the image of all the good things a man should be. He will be strong in body and character; he will be athletic as a youth, and competitive as an adult; he will be master of his house and defender of his group; and most of all, his behavior will be distinct from the behavior of women. The college athlete who becomes a war hero is the perfect positive role model for male children.

Children are also provided with a second kind of role model, the image of a man who is a failure. This is the major function of the homosexual stereotype. The stereotype of the gay man shows children what an incompetent man is like. He's a sissy at sports; he's interested in things that girls like; he's not competitive; he doesn't want to fight with other boys; and most damaging of all—he doesn't insist on his male prerogatives. He is the perfect contrast to the positive role model.

These two role models, the hero and the homosexual, teach the young boy what "being a man" is all about. If he patterns his behavior on that of the hero, the boy learns he will be rewarded. If he patterns it after the homosexual, he learns that he will be punished. By identifying with the hero, the boy increases his self-esteem; by identifying with the homosexual, he lowers it. The stereotype provides sanctions against the boy if he should prefer behavior that is not considered "masculine" in this society. At a very early age the boy learns that it is more to his credit for him to hit another boy who wounds his pride than to admit his hurt feelings. The stereotype has little to do with sexual behavior per se. Instead, it is society's prophylactic against someone who might dissolve the behavioral boundaries between boys and girls.

The old and rigid concept of masculinity seems to be breaking down these days, and many of us feel that our society will be stronger when a more humane definition of masculinity prevails. Some people suggest that androgyny, discussed in a previous chapter, will replace the old concepts of masculine and feminine. At the moment it might be interesting to consider how the old, rigid sex roles came about in the first place. There must have been a reason why they arose and why they have been adhered to for so long. I would like to suggest one theory.

During most of recorded history women were not the subject of any serious attention. They were necessary to bear children, had responsibility for the home, and monopolized early child rearing. Well-born women were pawns of their families or their king, and marriages were a principal means of cementing relationships between families or countries. If two families wished to combine their wealth, the daughter of one was contracted to marry the son of the other. No one was concerned about love or personal feelings. These things had no connection with marriage. The idea of loving one's spouse did not even occur to most people, and marriages for love were considered foolish at best. There are still many places in the world where marriage continues to be a matter of property and responsibility, and not a matter of personal choice.

For thousands of years the men in warlike tribes spent little time in the company of their wives. They were engaged in their main occupation, ensuring their tribes' survival. In those days, famine, disease and invaders constantly threatened them with destruction. Domestic skills and the conversation of uneducated women did not interest noblemen who negotiated treaties or warriors engaged in endless battles.

Power was admired. It could be gained through wealth or service, but for a long time it was concentrated in the hands of the military aristocracy. To defend their own castles successfully and to attack and overwhelm those of their neighbors were the duties of the powerful. Women could have only a minor role in such a society.

In most cases men preferred the company of other men to that of women. Sexually, they generally preferred their wives, or other women, but most of their time was spent with their comrades. In these early societies something that sociologists call "male bonding" was very strong. The term refers to an emotional tie between two men that frequently includes feelings of love (though not necessarily sexual love) and that can be so strong that one may sacrifice his own life to save the other. Famous examples of male bonding include King David and Jonathan in the Bible and Achilles and Patroclus in Homer's *Iliad.*

— Men frequently slept together, embraced intimately, and cared for each other's bodies in ways that modern men might find shocking. They could do this because they thought of themselves as equals, partners with a high status in their society; but sexual conduct was a different matter. The sexual act was not considered a union of equals as we think of it today. Sexual equality is another new idea, and one that would have been almost incomprehensible to the ancients. To them sex was intimately connected with the idea of the subjugation of an inferior by a superior, and one of the partners was always an inferior, physically or symbolically.

That's why two men of equal status could share every intimate experience except a sexual one. They could have the most profound emotional ties to one another as long as they did not sexualize them. A sexual relationship between them would have meant that one or the other would be assigned an inferior role and suffer a loss of status or power. Men took these ideas very seriously indeed, believing that once such a thing occurred a man would lose his masculinity forever. To these men sex was characterized by domination and exploitation.

At the same time, the powerful could engage in numerous homosexual relationships. It was perfectly acceptable for an adult man to have sexual relations with a youth. A youngster, probably in his early teens, was not yet a man and could not forfeit status he did not yet have. The boy accepted the sexual role assigned to him by the man, a role usually assigned to women. By having sex with a youth, a man could have homosexual relations without violating the masculine standards of the warrior class.

As a matter of fact, sex between adult men and youngsters was required in some ancient groups. For example, the Greeks who settled in Sparta believed that the essence of a man's masculine spiritual power could be transmitted to a boy through anal intercourse. Any boy who hoped to become a warrior was required to develop a sexual relationship with an adult man.

Paradoxically, just the opposite was true if two grown men had anal intercourse. The dropping of semen in the boy symbolized his acquisition of masculinity, while in the adult man it symbolized his loss of masculinity.

Let's sum up these ancient attitudes and see whether they help explain something about the homosexual stereotype today. Masculinity and power were synonymous because men distinguished themselves in war. Women were considered inferior because they were unsuited to war. What we would call homosexual relationships were acceptable among males as long as one partner was not yet accepted in the company of men because of his youth. Among men of equal rank, male bonding was acceptable but sexual relations were not.

Except in regard to sex with youngsters, it's awesome how many of the ancient male attitudes toward sex are still going strong. Even today women are habitually defined in terms of their subordinate role in sexual relations. For many people, sex between a man and a woman is almost as much an exercise in domination and power as it was in ancient Greece. And any man who allows another man to use him sexually automatically loses his masculinity, just as the Greeks believed.

But things are changing! The old distinctions between men and women, perhaps necessary many years ago, are no longer useful today. Displays of masculine physical strength don't have the survival value they once did. Brains have overtaken brawn, and battles are fought with ideas. Perhaps because our survival is less threatened than in the past, people are beginning to recognize that gay men are just as manly as other men—and that lesbians are no more or less womanly than other women It's part of the change in all of us as sexual beings.

chapter thirteen

MEDICINE AND MORALITY

This chapter and the next are devoted to answering one very important question: Is homosexuality a mental illness? We already know that in the past being gay has been perceived as a sin and a crime. In this century psychiatrists popularized the idea that being gay is a mental illness requiring treatment. For the first sixty or so years of the twentieth century, psychiatrists working with homosexuals had only one goal, to change them into heterosexuals.

In the course of the last twenty years, however, some mental health specialists have taken a good look at their work and have reevaluated the scientific basis of these ideas. They have become aware of how much their professional judgments have been influenced by morality. In a number of instances perfectly normal behavior has been judged abnormal and treated. Only later did these specialists realize that the "cure" was the problem, not the behavior. We can distinguish five steps in the transformation from normality to abnormality.

1. *The normal behavior:* First, the behavior violates social rules. In sexual matters, religious beliefs most commonly provides the basis for legal and social sanctions. Masturbation is a good example.

2. *The behavior is labeled "abnormal."* Psychologists and psychiatrists, influenced by moral beliefs, claim the behavior is abnormal. They say that it is a mental illness that can and should be cured by medical means. Masturbation was at one time considered abnormal, and physicians recommended that it can be cured.

3. *The label is internalized.* This step is of primary importance. Here the individual (in our example, the masturbator) must accept the judgment of the physician. S/he must come to the conclusion that his or her behavior is really an indication of mental illness, and must want to be cured. This is usually accomplished through indoctrination by educational institutions.

4. *Treatment:* The person now goes to the physician to be cured of the illness (masturbation). The object of the treatment is to make the person conform to social rules and taboos regarding sexual behavior. In this case, the person must be made to stop masturbating.

5. *Results of treatment:* The final result of this process is a person who is worse off than before, as the treatment causes more problems than the original complaint. (As I have noted, this is called an iatrogenic disorder.) There are two aspects to the harm done. First the person is conditioned to believe he is abnormal; then the treatment reinforces his poor attitude toward himself and uses some form of punishment that harms him even further.

I believe gay people can develop fully productive lives. They need have no problem with their sexuality, or at least no greater problem than heterosexuals have with theirs. The labeling as abnormal and the treatments that gays have been subjected to have always been unfair and harmful.

At the moment we are a society in flux. We've been changing a great deal lately, but it is still exceedingly difficult for us to examine our own prejudices objectively. It might be useful to consider a similar situation in the past that can provide us with parallels to the current controversy about homosexuality. Fortunately we can do this fairly easily. The history of medical opinion on masturbation furnishes us with the perfect example. A widespread and innocuous sexual practice, condemned as sinful on religious and moral grounds, masturbation was diagnosed as medically abnormal and treated by physicians. Nowadays we accept it as normal sexual behavior.

The basic premise of this chapter is that the controversy over whether homosexuality is an illness constitutes a direct parallel to the argument about masturbation. Let us now discuss how in the preceding century masturbators were condemned as abnormals and treated for their abnormality, and how homosexuals suffer the same fate today.

Masturbatory Insanity*

The medical writers of the eighteenth and nineteenth centuries were children of their generation just as you and I are children of ours. Science was then relatively new, and physicians could hardly explain the origin of most diseases, still less cure them. Throughout most of the history of medicine, physicians struggled to identify the physical causes of disease. They faced stiff competition from those who explained it in supernatural or moral terms.

These physicians lived in a period when prohibitions against sexual expression defined by religious authorities were still unquestioned. As children they were taught that any sexual act that did not result in pregnancy and childbirth was unnatural, and though many disagreed with other parts of church teaching, they still accepted its sexual morality as the standard of natural behavior. Because of this, their work in sexuality is a

*See Szasz, T. S. *The Manufacture of Madness.* New York: Dell Publishing Co., Inc., 1970, for a fine review of this story and its relation to homosexuality.

curious amalgamation of early scientific principles and religious dogma. They observed sexual behavior in their own society and explained it in religious terms, though they used fashionably scientific terminology. "Masturbatory insanity" underlies the whole nineteenth century conception of sexuality and has had an immense influence on our view of homosexuality as well.

It is almost impossible for people today to believe that "masturbatory insanity," a disease that terrorized people from the middle of the eighteenth century until the beginning of the twentieth, ever existed at all. Even so, some people can remember warnings against masturbation they heard as children. Stories that masturbation will cause hair to grow on your palms, or soften your brain, are thought of as jokes now. These old wives' tales were used to prevent children from engaging in what was once called "self-abuse." They are only faint echoes of the anti-masturbation crusade that physicians once approved and directed.

It began with a publication in 1758 called *Onania, Or a Treatise Upon the Disorders Produced by Masturbation.** It was written by a Swiss physician named Tissot. He believed that the loss of semen during sexual intercourse was injurious to the body. If a man engaged in sex too often, and consequently ejaculated too frequently, the depletion of his seminal fluid would cause a number of grave physical problems. These included consumption, pimples, tumors, constipation, hemorrhoids, blindness and early death. Another outcome of frequent ejaculation, he said, was insanity.

In order to prevent all these dire consequences, men were encouraged to hold on to their semen as long as possible. In other words, it should be used only for the

*English translation by A. Hume. London, J. Pridden, 1766.

purpose of reproduction. Masturbation, thereafter called "onanism," included every sexual act that did not lead to reproduction. Tissot's new word replaced the older term, "sodomy." Though the terminology changed, the idea remained the same.

Tissot didn't forget to include the dangers to which women were subject if they became sexually excited too often, though in those days almost any sexual excitement in women was "too often." They too were subject to the most serious physical disorders, including all those that affected men and, in addition, an underlying moral depravity that, unchecked, would reduce them to the level of animals.

Tissot also maintained that *masturbation destroyed the nervous system*, and that young people were particularly liable to be damaged in this way. If one's nervous system was destroyed, insanity would result. Tissot closed his text by concluding that the masturbator deserved our contempt. He would be punished by disease in this world and eternal fire in the next. These ideas, enlarged upon from time to time, remained scientific dogma for the next two centuries, and attenuated remnants of them are still with us today.

Masturbation was condemned by medical practitioners just as it had been condemned by religious authorities. Nineteenth-century medical writers were certain that masturbation explained a host of problems, both physical and social, and made every effort to stamp it out. Here are two typical quotations from important physicians of that day.

An editorial in the *New Orleans Medical and Surgical Journal*, 1854–1855:

> In my opinion, neither plague, nor war, nor smallpox nor a crowd of similar evils, have resulted more

disastrously for humanity than the habit of masturbation; it is the destroying element of civilized society [Quoted in Szasz, op. cit.; 186].

The French physician Pouillet wrote in 1876:

Of all the vices and of all the misdeeds which may properly be called crimes against nature, which devour humanity, menace its physical vitality and tend to destroy its intellectual and moral faculties, one of the greatest and most widespread—no one will deny it—is masturbation [Szasz, op. cit., p. 187].

What remarkable statements these are. Physicians claimed not only that masturbation caused the deterioration of the nervous system, but that it might destroy society. Most important is the transformation of the religious idea that sexual pleasure is sinful into a medical theory that it is physically harmful. It was nothing more than the Christian sexual ethic translated into the language of medicine.

In 1834 an American, Sylvester Graham,* wrote that the loss of an ounce of semen was equivalent to the loss of many ounces of blood. Every time a man ejaculated, he exposed himself to nervous disease and early death. Like Plato, he recommended that even married men not have sex more than twelve times a year or nervous damage would result. Graham could only imagine what might happen if a man indulged himself to excess! Any right-minded person would also stay away from pornography and erotic stories, since they encouraged ejaculation.

Graham believed that by eating the proper foods one could control the sexual energy that, released, would

*Graham, S. *A Lecture to Young Men, on Chastity, Intended also for the Serious Consideration of Parents and Guardians.* (10th Ed.) Boston: C. H. Pierce, 1848.

lead to insanity. Graham crackers were the solution! Graham flour was meant to provide a food that would dampen male erotic desires and lessen the temptation to masturbate.

In 1882, John Harvey Kellogg,* another American, was the next exponent of the theory of masturbatory insanity. He was the man who made the Battle Creek Sanatorium famous. Like Graham, he taught that the shock to the nervous system produced by masturbation, or indeed any sexual activity, was profoundly injurious. Some sexual activity was necessary for reproduction, but masturbation could never be excused. His endless list of disorders caused by masturbation included insanity, cancer, shifty eyes, epilepsy, a fondness for eating plaster and mock piety.

To fight the epidemic of masturbation, Kellogg invented foods for children that would reduce their inclination to self-abuse. This tradition soon made cereals the breakfast food of children. I wonder how many parents today ever dreamed that cereal was meant to lower their children's sex drive. The universal use of cereals as breakfast foods for children indicates how seriously parents were once concerned about the dangers of masturbation.†

Some parents also subjected their children to the most ingenious and painful restraints. Various physicians invented restraining devices into which children were nightly strapped or chained to prevent their hands from touching any part of their bodies. This was a very serious business in those days. But, though boys were

*Kellogg, J. H. *Plain Facts for Young and Old.* Burlington, Iowa: I. F. Segner, 1882. (Republished: Buffalo, Heritage Press, 1974.)

†See an excellent short review of this subject in Bullough, Vern L., "Homosexuality and the Medical Model." *Journal of Homosexuality*, vol. I, 1974, 99–110.

chastised or had their penises painted as punishment for masturbation, the repression of women's sexual desires is even more bizarre.

Masturbation as an Iatrogenic Disorder in Women

In the course of the nineteenth century, physicians placed greater and greater emphasis on the physiological origin of women's mental disorders. They classified masturbation, the desire for contraception and, incredibly enough, orgasm as symptoms of these mental disorders. This must be emphasized: for a woman to have an orgasm, or to desire one, during sexual intercourse was a sign of mental disorder. Treatment for such symptoms followed quickly.

Physicians claimed that a woman could be cured of her dangerous sexual perversity by surgery. The removal of part or all of the clitoris was all that was required! Cliterodectomy began in 1858, and the practice continued until the early twentieth century. Circumcision (removal of part or all of the hood) later replaced cliterodectomy as a treatment for female masturbators, and was so employed until 1937.

These operations were performed in an attempt to reimpose the traditional female role that our society felt was at stake. Men were fully sexual beings and needed orgasmic release—though if not held in check, this need could lead to the degeneration of the nervous system and eventual insanity. Women, on the other hand, were not perceived as having sexual needs at all. Nature meant them to satisfy their husbands and bear children abundantly. Any effort a woman made to break out of her traditional family role was interpreted by men as an insane attempt to usurp the natural rights and prerogatives of males. Many operations upon the female genitalia were performed to "cure" the woman's desire to be a man—proof of which was her desire to experience orgasm. This is not a proud page in our cultural history.*

Homosexuality as an Iatrogenic Disorder

The parallels between masturbatory insanity and the "disease" called homosexuality are very revealing, and those professionals who still maintain their belief in the latter are careful to forget that the former was ever supposed to exist at all.

In this century gays have been diagnosed as mentally ill and frequently confined to mental institutions, because psychiatrists have believed such institutions to be more suitable than prisons. Gays have usually believed otherwise, since a convicted criminal retains many of his civil rights, while a mental patient loses his. A prisoner leaves his jailhouse at the end of his sentence, but a mental patient leaves only when the psychiatrist gives his okay, often a capricious decision.

In the 1930's a new surgical technique called "lobotomy" was invented. This is a neurosurgical operation that *removes a large part of the brain.* It was very popular, and neurosurgeons claimed it could cure all manner of emotional problems. It actually turned the patient into a vegetable. It may have "cured" homosexuality, but this was sometimes at a cost of paralysis, inability to function in the outside world and, in some cases, death. Some lobotomized patients are still lying in the back wards of our mental institutions, where they will remain until they die.

A variation of lobotomy is the surgical insertion of electrodes in the brain of the gay man. The electrodes are connected to an electric circuit, and every time he feels

*This subject is treated poignantly in Barker-Benfield, B., "Sexual Surgery in Late-Nineteenth-Century America." *International Journal of Health Sciences,* 5, 1975, pp. 279–298.

homosexual desires, electricity is conducted through the electrode and into the brain. It is very unpleasant.*

Less dramatic than these surgical interventions but far more common in practice is psychoanalysis, considered by many the treatment of choice for homosexuals. Psychoanalysis involves a patient-therapist relationship in which the patient tries to understand the motivations of his behavior. This is the theory that states that parents cause the homosexuality of their child. It is the theory that has contributed to making many innocent parents feel guilty about their son or daughter's homosexuality. There is no evidence that this theory is correct, and a great deal of evidence that indicates it is not. Through countless years (and at a cost of thousands of dollars), the gay person is asked to analyze his or her "compulsive sexual desires." Since these therapeutic sessions almost always end in failure, the gay person comes to believe that s/he is a hopeless case.

In the past few years the methods for treating homosexuals (that is to say, methods for reorienting their sexual preference) have changed considerably. One of the new techniques most commonly used is called aversion therapy.

In aversion therapy the gay person is given a painful jolt of electricity as punishment for homosexual responses. In this procedure a gay man is shown slides of attractive nude men and women. Attached to his penis is a device that records sexual excitement. If he becomes sexually excited by the image of an attractive man he is jolted with electricity. When the pictures of women are shown, he is not shocked.

A variation uses fantasies instead of pictures. The gay man is instructed to imagine a sexual scene with

*For those who may believe that such primitive practices are a thing of the past, see Heath, R. G., "Pleasure and Brain Activity in Man." *Journal of Nervous and Mental Diseases*, 154, 1972, pp. 3–18.

another man. He is then told to imagine vomiting all over himself and the other man. The idea in both these forms of behavior therapy is to associate homosexuality with unpleasant experiences.

Yet another type of aversive conditioning has been used to change a person's sexual preference extensively. Drugs are substituted for electric shock. Injected into the bloodstream, these cause a violent reaction in the body, and for a few minutes the man is incapable of controlling his own respiration. Many patients have thought they were about to die.

There is still another, more up-to-date technique for changing a gay person's sexual preference. It has come upon the scene only in the last year or two, and it promises to be widely used. It is the use of anti-androgen drugs. If you think back to Henry Burke's "cure," you will remember that he was given testosterone, one of the male sex hormones. Collectively, the male hormones are called androgens. All androgens are normally produced in the body and influence our sexual desires.

An anti-androgen drug, when injected into the body, either neutralizes the sex hormone normally produced, or prevents its production. In effect, it causes the person to become asexual, which is the condition desired by these psychiatrists. Some psychiatrists maintain that we keep people asexual for the rest of their lives with maintenance doses of these drugs. Others have higher goals. They propose to use the asexual period to "retrain" the gay man to be heterosexual. The psychiatrists hope that after he learns to eschew homosexual experiences and to desire heterosexual ones the injections can be terminated.*

There is controversy among this group of psychia-

---

*Most of these treatments are reviewed in Sansweet, S. J., *The Punishment Cure.* New York, Mason/Charter, 1975.

trists about how to accomplish sexual reorientation during the asexual period. So far they have been unsuccessful, but they are still determined to continue, stating that they have a duty to help patients who desire sexual reorientation. Some go so far as to say that even if they don't achieve a heterosexual orientation, asexuality is better than homosexuality.

There are other professionals, this psychologist included, who are horrified at the behavior of physicians who claim for themselves the power to control our lives in such profound ways. In terms of civil liberties, the potential for mischief is obvious, and many civil rights groups are beginning to raise their voices against the promiscuous use of these drugs. It seems to parallel the treatment accorded to women in the nineteenth century. Just as women then were punished for their sexual desires, so gays are being punished for their sexual desires today. In both cases it is immoral and improper treatment.

chapter fourteen

MEDICINE AND HOMOSEXUALITY

There was a time when gay people were forced into psychiatric treatment. Judges would commonly tell the convicted gays that they could either go into treat' ment or go to jail, and many accepted treatment. Enforced treatment has now been rejected by the professional community both for therapeutic reasons and because of the potential infringements on civil rights. The accepted ethical standards in the professions of psychiatry and psychology state that a therapist should treat a patient only if he voluntarily asks for treatment. No coercion is allowed. Therefore most (unfortunately not all) professionals would be against forcing a gay person into treatment to change his sexual preference. These same professionals would also state that sexual reorientation should be attempted *if the gay person voluntarily asks for it.*

This has a familiar ring. It is the same argument used by surgeons in the nineteenth century when defending their circumcision of women. But if women's circumcision for masturbation was an iatrogenic procedure, causing harm to women, the current treatments for homosexuality may also be harmful to gay people. This is the controversy that exists in the professional community at this time.

171

Women as Voluntary Patients for Circumcision. Incredible as it may now seem, women welcomed circumcision. They were conditioned by male authorities to believe that their nervous systems were particularly sensitive, and that they had to make a much greater effort than men in order to prevent overexcitement or overstimulation. A woman knew that experiencing sexual excitement or—worse yet—an orgasm, or desiring contraception or abortion were symptoms of mental illness.

Most women in the nineteenth century insisted that they be restored to their proper role in society as sexually unresponsive, dependent and submissive beings. Women did not object to circumcision, or cliterodectomy, or even to ovariotomy when that was the favored treatment for masturbation. *Women were voluntary subjects for the surgeons.* One example will suffice.

Dr. E. W. Cushing, a noted Boston surgeon at the end of the nineteenth century, performed innumerable circumcisions upon women *who begged him* for the operation. One woman who had been circumcised in order to extirpate masturbatory desires wrote after the operation:

> My condition is all I could desire. I know and feel that I am well; I never think of self-abuse; it is foreign and distasteful to me. A window has been opened to heaven [Barker-Benfield, op. cit., p. 293].

This woman had been taught that her genitals were filthy, and that masturbation was a violation of her role as wife and mother, a sin in the eyes of God, and a sure sign that degenerative insanity would sooner or later condemn her to an asylum.

Indeed the record shows that some physicians tried to avoid these operations. Yet if the women themselves demanded them, were physicians not committed to relieving the pain and suffering these women complained of so strongly? Some women even committed suicide as a result of the self-hatred and guilt induced by masturbation.

Can we accuse the physician of improper treatment if the patient demands that treatment? Even if the treatment is hazardous, should the physician refuse it if the patient understands the hazards and still demands the cure? There are a number of professionals and laymen who believe that women should not have been circumcised, no matter how desperately they may have begged for it. These critics say that medicine should never be used in the service of repression. The doctor's role should be confined to curing physical illness. Doctors should not use their skills to enforce social customs. Some adherents of the women's liberation movement see the circumcision of women as but one example of the use of medicine to punish women and keep them in their subservient roles. In this view, the surgeons were instruments of tyranny.

Other physicians (and also psychologists and psychiatrists) disagree. They reply to their critics by saying that physicians and psychotherapists have no right to choose the goals for treatment for their patients. Each day they face the human pain and misery of patients who beg for help. How can they refuse? How could the surgeons of the last century have refused their patients, and damned them to depression, marital unhappiness and possibly suicide? They argue further that refusing treatment would be an imposition of their beliefs on others. Wouldn't such a refusal be just as immoral? These are powerful arguments, and they cannot be ignored.

The really crucial question is this: What is a voluntary patient? If women who were taught to suppress their sexuality asked for surgery, were they acting voluntarily? Couldn't one say that no one can be considered a voluntary patient for any treatment unless s/he understands why s/he wants the treatment, as well as the hazards the treatment entails? And let us suppose a patient does understand that his or her request for treatment is motivated by a desire to conform to the rest of society. Is the doctor obligated to provide the treatment even though there is nothing physically wrong? Can the treatment be refused because it violates the doctor's moral beliefs?

This is a very difficult question. With sufficient conditioning, a person will come to believe that his or her behavior is sick and go for the cure. Women were conditioned from the time they were little girls to believe that *they were normal if they had no sexual feeling*. At that point the medical concept of "normality" became hopelessly confused with moral and social rules, which have nothing to do with medicine at all.

The dilemma is solved only when we decide whether it is the attitude or the behavior that is "sick." In other words, were women unhappy because they were deprived of their sexuality, or because they experienced sexuality?

If physicians agreed that women should be allowed full sexual expression, then their responsibility could only have been to try to change women's attitudes. But this course would have put doctors in the position of attacking an important moral rule. If physicians had raised their voices against the prevailing repressive attitude toward women, they would have hastened the freedom of women. As it was, their silence was support for the status quo.

Homosexuals as Voluntary Patients for Sexual Reorientation. I've spent so much time discussing masturbatory insanity because its history shows how carefully we must consider whether our diagnoses and treatments help or hurt our patients. The current argument about the treatment for homosexuality is exactly the same as that raised by the nineteenth century's treatment of female sexuality.

First, let me state the most important fact. The overwhelming majority of gay people have never wanted, nor do they now want, to change their sexual preference. Lesbians in particular have never volunteered for any treatment that would interfere with their life-style. But some gay men have been extremely upset about their homosexuality, and these men have offered themselves for treatment. They are the exact counterparts of the women who offered themselves for circumcision years before. Like the women, their problem has been their attitude toward themselves, carefully engendered by years of training.

As a rule, these men are troubled and depressed. They suffer from low self-esteem, and they attribute all their problems in life to their sexual preference. Here is their typical life pattern: At an early age, the boy learns that his father has certain manly expectations, and if he does not fulfill them, he disappoints his father. Strike one! In elementary school he discovers that he does not conform to his age-mates' and elders' idea of a boy. He's a "sissy." Strike two! As he gets older he learns words like "queer" and "fag," and begins to understand the contempt shown by the use of these words, and he starts to wonder whether he is contemptible. Strike three! In church he learns that he is a sinner, and the more religious he is, the more he believes it. Strike four! Then he finds out that "queers" are mentally ill. Strike five! Then he learns that being a "fag" is also against the law! Strike six!

And all the time he hides his feelings. He pretends to be interested in women, but he really uses them only to hide behind, and he hates himself for the deception. He doesn't become acquainted with other gay people because he thinks that they are degenerate and sick. These judgments are really feelings about himself projected onto an unknown world that frightens him. And he reads books written by people who encourage his feelings of guilt, and he feels worse still.

Above all, he feels guilty about his sexual desires. Every time he experiences a homosexual urge, all the negative judgments of his family and community return to haunt him. No one need say them to him any more. He had learned to say these things to himself:

"I am a disappointment."
"I am a queer."
"I am a fag."
"I am a sinner."
"I am a criminal."
"I am sick."
"I am a pervert."
"I am guilty of all these things, therefore I am unworthy."

This kind of gay man has never experienced love for another man, nor does he believe it possible. Since he isolates himself from other gays, he feeds on himself, each day diminishing what little self-respect he has, until he believes in nothing but his own depravity.

Guilty men should be punished. The kind of gay man I have pictured so vividly looks for a way to ease his pain. Punishing himself for his sins or crimes is the only way he can find to allay his guilt. To him the cure is the punishment he deserves for the crime of desiring the wrong person. Psychoanalysis reinforces his guilt. Aversion therapy and the use of drugs punish him more directly and painfully. But these treatments do not "cure" him of anything.

I do not believe that this kind of man is a "volunteer" for sexual reorientation. I do not believe his choice is made freely. He does have problems, and severe ones, but homosexuality is not one of them. His chief problem is his denial of his own sexual preference, and his attempts to punish himself for his desires.

I do not believe that professionals should punish their patients, nor do I believe that they should agree to change a person's sexual preference. I can see no difference between the punishment of masturbation in the nineteenth century and the punishment of homosexuality in the twentieth. In the seventeenth century, they punished sexual non-conformism with death; in the eighteenth with castration; in the nineteenth with asylums; and now in the twentieth we use psychotherapy or aversion therapy. This is not done in the interest of the patient. *It is the patient who is taught to serve our interest.*

Changing Psychological Opinion on Masturbation. In the past fifty years the sexual attitudes of our society have changed, and the attitudes of the medical and psychological professions have altered to fit our new morality. In the middle years of this century masturbation was still considered a sexual perversion, though it was no longer believed to lead to insanity. Psychiatric authorities claimed that masturbation interfered with the development of normal sexual relations. They recommended psychiatric treatment to cure the child, or adult, of his or her "self-abuse."

Until 1968 masturbation was still officially an abnormal form of behavior, classified as such in the diagnostic manual of the American Psychiatric Association. By this time, however, it was obvious to the members of the association that this classification of masturbation could no longer be maintained by any group that also laid claim to rationality and scientific accuracy.

Studies such as Kinsey's had shown that more than ninety percent of the male population was suffering from this abnormality.

Then in 1968 masturbation, in itself, was removed from the psychiatrists' list of mental disorders. But old views die very hard. According to the new classification, masturbation is a mental illness only if it is excessive. How one is to judge whether masturbation is excessive is left obscure.

Ironically, today many professionals use masturbation as a therapeutic technique in the treatment of sexual dysfunctions. What was once unanimously held to be a fatal degenerative disease is now considered one of the most effective methods of helping people solve their sexual problems. It is accepted as a normal form of sexual activity and is no longer even mildly controversial. Orgasm, which was once one of the most serious symptoms of masturbatory insanity in women, is now a sign of a healthy sexual life and a desirable goal in therapy. Many women who have never experienced orgasm register at sexual dysfunction clinics, and masturbation is the most important technique that therapists use to assist them in achieving orgasm.

Changing Psychological Opinion on Homosexuality. In the past twenty years psychologists and psychiatrists have attempted to find differences in the emotional health of gay and heterosexual people. They have done this by giving each group a standardized test and comparing the results. After scores of comparisons, psychologists have concluded that there are no differences between the two groups. Gays are just as healthy, and just as unhealthy, as heterosexuals. This includes gay men as well as lesbians. In a way, it's remarkable that gays have fared so well emotionally, considering the amount of discrimination they experience.

This important research was ignored for years by the psychiatric establishment. It refused to alter its theories, and continued to apply the label "abnormal" to all non-reproductive sexual behavior. "Abnormal" continued to be a synonym for "sodomy."

In 1968 the American Psychiatric Association revised its diagnostic handbook, and with it its classification of homosexuality. Homosexuality was removed from the category of "psychopathy," and placed under the new heading "sexual deviations." Into this new classification were placed all the varieties of sexual behavior that society condemned, including men masturbating in women's underwear, peeping toms, exhibitionism, masochism and even necrophilia. This was considered an improvement by the psychiatrists. While in 1942 the homosexual was classified as a "psychopath"—a person who commits violent crimes—in 1968 the homosexual was grouped with people who force their unusual sexual desires on others. Instead of helping homosexuals, the psychiatric establishment was turning its power against them.

These diagnostic labels influenced our laws. The sodomy laws that still exist in most states use many of the terms from the psychiatric handbook as justification for imprisoning gay people. In many states gay people are still legally defined as perverts, psychopaths, or sexual deviants. The diagnostic labels of the psychiatrists have further reinforced discrimination against gay people.

But by the early nineteen-seventies, the research studies could no longer be ignored. These studies could find no abnormality in gay people, and many professionals started to realize how much their previous theories of homosexuality had been based on social conformity. Many of the psychiatrists asked for a revision of the diagnosis as a first step in righting their error.

At the same time, an important change occurred

within the gay community. This was the rise of the gay liberation movement. It began with the raid on the Stonewall in New York City (discussed in Chapter Ten). After the Stonewall, a number of gay people decided to organize into groups to fight discriminatory attitudes. It was obviously the right moment, for thousands of people joined the organizations that developed during the late sixties and early seventies. For the first time, large numbers of gay people came out of the closet, met and talked with other gays. They organized around the issue of civil rights, and they directed all their energies against any discriminatory institution that interfered with equal rights for gay people.

The therapeutic value of being a part of the gay liberation movement was enormous. Large numbers of gay people marched publicly in the streets. They faced the television cameras and newspaper photographers. They were interviewed by reporters. It was the first time they came out publicly—and they liked it. They felt proud to work with other gays, and they did so effectively.

Many of them found that marching through the streets did more to restore their pride than years of psychotherapy. They expressed their anger and outrage toward the police, against the lawmakers and against employers. The feeling of solidarity was bound to make important psychological changes.

They protested the use of brutal treatment techniques, and brought their opposition to the home grounds of the psychiatrists and psychologists. They marched into professional meetings and insisted that a gay person sit on any panel that discussed the use of aversive therapy or psychotherapy with gay people. They demanded that professionals explain why they tried to change sexual preference when their own research showed that gay people were not sick. They demanded to know why, if the gay person's problem was guilt and low self-esteem, they focused on changing sexual preference rather than on removing guilt and raising self-esteem.

When professionals claimed that they were only doing what their patients requested, gays reminded them that physicians of the last century said the same thing about women's masturbation. The silence of professionals in this century has been just as oppressive as the silence of physicians in the last one.

Many gays in the movement left their therapists. They no longer wanted to work with those who considered them sick. They sought out therapists who were themselves gay, and openly so. In many large cities there are a number of these gay therapists who offer more honest therapeutic services to gay people, and gay people are right to go to them.

Various organizations of the gay liberation movement insisted that their voices be heard on the harm of psychiatric diagnosis. They insisted that the psychiatric establishment face up to the research that clearly indicated the error of labeling gay people "sick." They also wanted professionals to take some of the responsibility for the repressive laws that sentenced gay people to prison for consentual sexual acts.

Activists in the gay liberation movement and a large number of professionals joined forces to oppose the diagnosis of homosexuality as a sickness. Many professionals already realized that this was only a modern medical guise for the old conception of "sodomy," and they too opposed the use of medicine for social control. Some very eminent members of the professional community spoke out for change. The American Psychiatric Association could no longer ignore the chorus of advocates who claimed that medicine had been used to hurt people instead of helping them.

In February 1973 the Nomenclature Committee of

the American Psychiatric Association invited a group of gay people to present the case for removing homosexuality from the list of disorders in the association's official diagnostic manual. The presentation included the research that showed no abnormality in homosexuals, and explained how the "sick label" had caused emotional problems for gay people.

In December 1973 the Board of Trustees of the American Psychiatric Association voted unanimously to remove homosexuality from their list of disorders. They decided that homosexuality was a disorder only if the gay person was in conflict about it. Such people were thenceforth to be diagnosed as having a "sexual orientation disturbance." "This diagnostic category," says the new manual, "is distinguished from homosexuality, which by itself does not necessarily constitute a psychiatric disorder."*

The statement issued by the Board of Trustees of the American Psychiatric Association went much further:

> Whereas homosexuality in and of itself implies no impairment in judgment, stability, reliability, or vocational capabilities, therefore, be it resolved that the American Psychiatric Association deplores all private and public discrimination against homosexuals in such areas as employment, housing, public accommodations, and licensing, and declares that no burden of proof of such judgment, capacity, or reliability shall be placed upon homosexuals greater than that imposed on any other persons. Further, the American Psychiatric Association supports and urges the enactment of civil rights legislation at local, state, and federal levels that would insure homosexual citizens the same protections now guar-

*American Psychiatric Association press release, December 15, 1973.

anteed to others; further the American Psychiatric Association supports and urges the repeal of all legislation making criminal offenses of sexual acts performed by consenting adults in private.*

This far-ranging statement was highly praised by many people. But there were a number of psychiatrists who deplored the action. Those who opposed the diagnostic change demanded that the entire national membership be polled. If the member psychiatrists of the American Psychiatric Association disagreed with the actions of the Board of Trustees, the diagnostic changes would have to be rescinded.

The membership was polled in 1974. They voted overwhelmingly to approve the diagnostic change, and "homosexuality" was permanently removed from the list of disorders in the American Psychiatric Association diagnostic manual. Evidently most psychiatrists have now come to believe that homosexuality in itself does not constitute a mental illness.

In 1975 the American Psychological Association, the largest professional association of psychologists in the United States, responded to the actions of the psychiatrists by announcing that:

The governing body of the American Psychological Association today voted to oppose discrimination of homosexuals and to support the recent action by the American Psychiatric Association which removed homosexuality from that association's list of mental disorders.†

But the psychologists went a bit further than the psychiatrists, for they urged "all mental health professionals to take the lead in removing the stigma of mental

*American Psychiatric Association press release, December 15, 1973.
†American Psychological Association press release, January 24, 1975.

illness that has long been associated with a homosexual orientation."* This last sentence was an important admission from the psychologists, that labeling people can cause harm where none existed before.

The next year, Dr. Gerald Davison,† president of the Association for the Advancement of Behavior Therapy, recommended that all behavior therapists terminate their programs for changing homosexuals into heterosexuals. He opposed such treatments on both moral and therapeutic grounds.

And in a recent issue of the *Journal of Homosexuality*, Dr. Kurt Freund,†† one of the pioneers in the use of aversion therapy for gay people, has announced that gays cannot be made into heterosexuals. After years of follow-up on his patients, Dr. Freund concluded that changes were transient at best.

Is homosexuality a mental illness? According to the statements of the American Psychiatric Association and the American Psychological Association, it is not. As a result of all the objective research by psychologists in the course of the past twenty years we now recognize that gay people suffer from the same kinds of problems as anyone else in our society, with the exception of problems that result from discrimination.

Clinical practice only confirms what research studies have indicated for so long: that gay people are not mentally ill. In New York City there is a special and independent psychotherapy clinic for gay men and women. It's called the Institute for Human Identity. As director of this clinic since its beginning in 1973, I have

*American Psychological Association press release, January 24, 1975.

†Davison, G. C. "Homosexuality: The Ethical Challenge," *Journal of Consulting and Clinical Psychology*, 1976, v. 44, 157–162.

††Freund, K. "Should Homosexuality Arouse Therapeutic Concern?" *Journal of Homosexuality*, 1977, v. 2, 235–240.

seen many hundreds of gay men and women seek our help. Frequently our patients apply for our services after long and unsatisfactory experience with other therapists, who insist on treating them as sick people.

What have we learned from this experience? We have found that gays can function as well as any other person in our society, if only they are not persecuted. Remarkably, even when the persecution continues, many gays will function well once they've learned to express their need for love and learned how to find it.

chapter fifteen

AN ALTERNATIVE FORM
OF THERAPY

Clearly gay men and women have problems, and they sometimes need professional help in solving them. Just as heterosexually married people sometimes need a marriage counselor to help them with marital conflicts, gay couples need professional help for the same reason. When a therapist recognizes that a gay couple can love each other as much as a heterosexual couple, he can address himself realistically to their problems. The capacity to love and care for another person is an individual quality. It has nothing to do with whether the other person is of the same or the opposite sex. Gays struggle with their need for love, and their fear of intimacy. They struggle with their determination to express pride in themselves, and their fear of retribution. They struggle with their desires for quiet middle-class respectability, and the need for political activism. Their struggles are the conflicts through which we all grow toward adult maturity. They are the conflicts of living in a complex modern world that has not made a place for gay love relationships.

I have worked with some gays who were upset about their homosexuality. They've asked for a "cure." This is what I told them:

"I believe that being gay is a natural way to be. People who are gay can love as well as anyone else, and except for the problems caused by discrimination, they can be as happy as anybody else. It all depends on whether you can learn to love and find another person who will love you in return.

"If you come into therapy with me, I will try to teach you how to love yourself and how to find someone to love you, but I do not believe that you should feel guilty about your sexual feelings. I'll try to stop you from hurting yourself, and I'll try to help you learn how to express your sexuality.

"If you have problems relating to the opposite sex, I'll try to help you feel more comfortable with them, but I won't try to cure you of your homosexuality, since it isn't an illness. If it turns out that you can find happiness through bisexuality, then that's a wonderful thing. I'm here to help enlarge your sexuality. If that's what you would like me to do, then let's begin."

This approach is not unique to me. It is the response of an ever larger number of psychologists and psychiatrists to requests for sexual reorientation. We feel that the goals of therapy in the past were misguided and influenced more by religious and social values than by concern for the eventual happiness of the patient. Our belief is that gay people are not ill and do not need treatment for their homosexuality. We work to help the gay person neutralize the old prejudiced attitudes and substitute the goal of making homosexuality an opportunity for personal growth.

In general terms, we try to take whatever guilt a gay person feels about being homosexual and turn that psychological energy into personal pride. We also redirect the energy bound up in low self-esteem into a new channel that leads to positive goals in life. Specifically, we work innovatively in the following seven areas. (In each case I will compare our approach with the negative forms of therapy and the differences between them will be obvious.)

1. Sex: The old form of therapy characterized gay people as oversexed individuals whose lust was uncontrollable. You may have noticed in the chapters on stereotypes, religion and the law that sex was what most concerned the outside world with regard to gay people. Attention was paid only to sexual acts, and not to the more important issue of loving and caring. Sex is only one aspect of gay relationships, but the old forms of therapy concentrated on sexuality and ignored the equally important need for love and companionship.

The new therapy tries to balance the gay person's need for sexual fulfillment with his or her need for intimate love relationships. Most of us feel lonely when we cannot share our lives with another person fully. Most of us want to experience that love for another person that provides meaning for human life. Sex is only one way of expressing love. The emphasis in our therapy is placed on finding a person to love and learning how to handle the personal vulnerability that results from caring about someone that much.

2. Isolation: The old form of therapy isolated gay people from one another. It counseled each individual gay person to avoid other gay people, lest he or she be encouraged to continue a homosexual life-style. Any attempt to seek reinforcement from other gay people was considered a "resistance" to therapy and proof of the patient's neurotic personality.

When the old therapies were still going strong, many gay people actually knew nothing about homosexuality except their own personal experience of it. They didn't know what other gay people were like or what kind of lives they led. Though most gays have to handle similar problems relating to the heterosexual world, an isolated gay person could not benefit from the experience of his peers.

The new form of therapy actively encourages the gay person to meet other gay people. Gay groups, whether political or social, are extremely important. They provide the support that is necessary to encourage pride. They are a place where hiding and defensiveness are unnecessary, and gay people can relax. They also permit gay people to learn about the lives of other gays and to develop friendships. We actively encourage our patients to find these gay groups and to participate in them. Their value is so great that they frequently result in quicker positive psychological change than years of psychotherapy. I have also seen cases where they have neutralized years of harmful psychotherapy.

3. Discrimination: Since the old form of therapy reinforced feelings of guilt, it encouraged gay people to accept their third-class status. While therapists have always claimed to be opposed to prejudice, their "sickness' label has always been one of the mainstays of the discrimination they claim to be against. Standing up for one's rights is difficult when you are being taught that you are a sinner, a lawbreaker and a mental patient! People lose self-respect when their civil rights are denied or abused, and they cannot speak out or fight back.

The new form of therapy tries to reverse this insidious process. It does not ask the gay person to suppress his or her outrage at discrimination, but allows that anger to be expressed. While the reality of a person's life may be that s/he cannot express that anger directly to the world, we recognize its validity. Sometimes the anger can be expressed in the security of gay groups, and when that is possible we encourage it.

4. Coming Out: The old form of therapy discouraged the gay person from coming out. In this context I am using "coming out" to mean being open about one's homosexuality. Since the old therapists were always hoping to change the person's sexual preference, coming out would have been counterproductive. Therapists always emphasized the dangers of coming out, the potential rejection by the family, the economic sanctions and all the penalties society inflicts on nonconformists.

The new form of therapy encourages gay people to look at both sides of the problem. You always pay a price when you stay in the closet. We examine that price, and the effects of deception and fraud. We also examine the potential rewards and hazards of being open about one's homosexuality. We suggest that our patients speak to other gays who have come out and learn about their experiences. In contrast to the therapists who discouraged coming out, we try to help the person weigh the advantages and disadvantages both of coming out and of remaining in the closet. It is a more balanced approach. The gay person must make his or her own choice and accept both the rewards and the penalties of the decision.

5. The Therapist: The old form of therapy always encouraged the patient to see a heterosexual therapist. Under no circumstances was a homosexual therapist—and there are many—considered appropriate. Since the old-school position claimed homosexuality was a mental illness, what good could be served by a patient working with a therapist who suffered from the same ailment?

The new form of therapy holds that a gay therapist can be an important asset in the treatment program. This is particularly true if the patient has been isolated from other gays in the past. If he or she has never had the opportunity to see a positive gay person, then an openly gay therapist may be one of the most excellent vehicles for bringing about positive change. The gay therapist becomes a role model for the patient.

6. Causes: The old form of therapy always looked for the cause of a person's homosexuality. Since being gay was considered abnormal, finding the cause was the therapist's first step in attempting a cure: sexual preference change. This emphasis intensified guilt, and it denied the possibility of a homosexual leading a rewarding life.

The new form of therapy believes that homosexuality is a natural sexual development. It also recognizes that we are no closer now to understanding the origin of heterosexual or homosexual preferences than we were one hundred years ago. We concentrate on making a person's sexual preference a positive attribute that can bring either pleasure or pain. We try to help the patient integrate his or her sexuality into a context of human relationships. We define abnormality in terms of how a person uses his or her natural attributes, and we do not make a moral judgment on the attributes themselves.

7. The Opposite Sex: The old form of therapy encouraged the patient to seek sexual relationships with the opposite sex as an antidote for homosexual desires. Gay men particularly used women either to sustain a pretense of normality or as a medium for retraining. Since this was generally done without the women's knowledge, it proved a rather complicated and confusing situation for the woman who was being used. It was as unfair to her as it was to the gay man, who more often than not had sex with the woman only to please his therapist.

The new form of therapy encourages a more honest relationship with the opposite sex. We attempt to help our patients appreciate the attractions of all kinds of people, and not cut themselves off from either sex. For gay people, having a sexual relationship with someone of the opposite sex is gratifying only when it is desired and not when it is part of a treatment. We encourage such contacts if the patient desires them.

There are clearly many differences between these two therapeutic approaches. Both of them are based on value judgments. One seeks to reinforce social expectations, while the other emphasizes the value of gay life and the means of attaining personal growth regardless of the prejudices of the outside world.

chapter sixteen

HOW TO CHOOSE
A THERAPIST

Psychotherapy is not magic. It's a long and difficult process in the course of which patient and therapist
touch on very sensitive feelings. Psychotherapy is an
educational experience. Patients learn to accept responsibility for themselves and train themselves in new and
more personally rewarding forms of behavior. Unless a
person is highly motivated, psychotherapy will fail. *Your*
son or daughter is the only one who can decide whether
to see a *psychotherapist.* The issue is not whether a
person needs help, but whether a person *wants* help. If
he or she does not, neither encouragement nor threats can
provide the motivation. In fact, they will probably have
the opposite effect.

I have seen many parents make an appointment
with a therapist for their child, only to learn to their
dismay that the child refuses to keep it. This is not an
easy lesson for most parents, because they feel frustrated
and hurt. They often look to the professional to bring the
child into psychotherapy, only to find that the therapist
too is resistant. The therapist knows that if the child does
not make the commitment to psychotherapy freely it will
be a useless exercise.

On countless occasions I have met with parents

who have just learned of their child's homosexuality. Still in a state of confusion, they have assumed that psychotherapy would be directed toward making the child heterosexual. This is a common request that must be refused. Though their intentions may be the best, parents cannot determine the goals of therapy for their children, nor can the therapist act as an agent of the parents. The goals of therapy can only be set by the patient and the therapist. If your child is comfortable with his homosexuality, he will not seek therapy to change it, nor should he. No responsible therapist would try to change him.

Some parents suggest therapy too quickly, often immediately upon finding out about the child's homosexuality. The child interprets this suggestion as a demand that his or her sexual preference be changed. This is, in fact, what most parents want when they ask the child to see a psychiatrist. Though parents may not understand it, most gays are perfectly happy with their life-style. If it is your intention to change your son or daughter's sexual preference, then you should expect to be rejected.

Nevertheless, there are ways you can be helpful. First of all you should allow a reasonable amount of time to pass after you have learned of your child's homosexuality. During this period you should talk with the child about his or her life and your concerns about it. Immediately referring the child to a psychiatrist is bound to be interpreted as meaning that you don't want to talk. If your child wants to talk to you, listen. At this stage your own family discussions are more valuable than any therapy. The strength in a family comes from working things out together, from listening to each other and caring for each other. Put the idea of professional help aside until this initial coming-out period has ended.

It often turns out that a child will ask for professional help, unprompted, in the course of one of these discussions. You need only meet the request, and help find a therapist if that is necessary. In other circumstances a child may be too shy to ask. Then parents must have a good sense of timing, and most parents do. If a child is feeling depressed or confused, the parents can bring up the possibility of therapy. If this is suggested with sensitivity, it is unlikely to be interpreted as meddling; but parents should be sure that they are making the suggestion on the child's behalf and not for their own sake. Even if the child refuses he will know that the suggestion was made for his benefit.

The therapy is your son or daughter's, not to yours. That means that the child must choose his or her own goals. These may be very different from the goals you would have set. In fact, many children want to enter psychotherapy to resolve their guilty feelings about homosexuality. They may want to use therapy to make themselves happier *as homosexuals.* This is their right. Their lives are their own, and each of them is going to live in his or her own way, regardless of what you want. If that is your child's goal, then that will be the direction of therapy. You will have to trust your child to make the best use of therapeutic experience.

Perhaps your son or daughter is not the one who should seek the help of a professional. Perhaps you should. There are some parents who become extremely depressed when they learn of their child's homosexuality. Sometimes this information is used by one parent against the other, or it is invested with guilt that the parent has always felt. I know of situations where the gay child is in good shape emotionally, while the parents are in turmoil. It would be foolish to insist that the gay children seek help when clearly the parents need it more.

Family therapy is an excellent way to deal with the problems of the gay child and the family. It also serves the parents well when their emotional distress interferes with their relationship with the children. If you feel guilty or resentful or angry or hurt by your child's homosexuality, then perhaps you should try family therapy.

The most difficult job of all is choosing a psychotherapist, either for yourself or your son or daughter. There needs to be a "good fit" between the personalities of the therapist and the patient. The right therapist is not always easy to find, but I can make a few suggestions that may help.

Once again, don't rush. Too many people hurry into psychotherapy. Choosing a psychotherapist is not something that should be done in a state of panic and anxiety. Unless there is the most acute crisis, such as a potential suicide, a good deal of thought is advisable in making such an important decision.

Find a qualified professional. This means a psychologist with a Ph.D. in psychology, a psychiatrist, who has an M.D., or a social worker with an M.S.W. degree. Many states have certification or licensing laws that insure that a licensed psychologist, psychiatrist, or social worker has been approved as qualified by the appropriate state agency. By all means ask the therapist about his professional background and whether or not s/he is licensed. It's not important which degree the therapist has. What is important is his or her training and experience as a therapist.

Secondly, the person who wants to go into therapy should interview more than one psychotherapist. Since you or your child will be placing your emotional life in the hands of this person, you should allow yourself to choose the therapist you feel most comfortable with. Some parents complain that this procedure is expensive and wasteful; but consider how much more money you will have wasted if after seeing a therapist for a year or more you discover that you've made a mistake! The only way to know whether you feel really comfortable with a therapist is to compare your reactions to two or more of them.

Since you will be discussing issues of sexuality, the therapist should be tolerant of the differences in people's sexual behavior, not the kind of person who has rigid ideas of what constitutes "proper" sexual behavior. The therapist who knows exactly what "normal" sexual behavior is should be avoided, as s/he might be motivated by a desire to make the patient conform.

Trust your own feelings about the therapist. If your son or daughter is seeking a therapist, suggest that they trust their own feelings. If you feel good in the therapist's presence, it's a good bet that you two will get along. If you don't, stay away, no matter how highly the therapist is recommended. Above all, do not choose or reject a therapist on the basis on the size of his or her fees. The price a therapist charges for services bears little or no relationship to the person's ability.

Other Sources of Help: Until now we have only considered going to a professional for help. Unfortunately, too many parents feel that only the professional psychologist or psychiatrist can aid them when they are confused or upset about a child's homosexuality. Sometimes a professional can be the wrong person to see.

Why do parents think of professionals so consistently? There are two reasons. In the first place, many parents feel embarrassed about discussing the subject of homosexuality, and they turn to someone who will respect the confidentiality of the material. They also assume that the psychologist or psychiatrist knows a great deal about the subject and will be able to explain the origin of their child's behavior and be able to cure it.

It is the second reason that carries more psychological weight. Parents have a long experience of guiding their children toward maturity. For years they have taught their children how to learn from their experience and how to create values for themselves. But by the time they are sexually mature, children are bound to experiment or choose sexual experiences that conflict with the values of their parents. Parents of gay children soon find that no matter what their view or opinion, the child will continue to live a gay sexual life. In this way, parents come to feel that they have lost control over the value system of their child. It is this loss of control—the inability of parents to guide the behavior of the child—that brings many into the consulting room.

What happens psychologically is that parents feel *helpless* to deal with the situation. Helplessness is a terrifying and lonely experience. When a person *feels* helpless (in contrast to really being helpless), he feels incompetent and inferior. These feelings immobilize a parent. Parents go to see the professional because they feel that they no longer have any influence over their child. Parents seek help from the professional because they cannot handle the situation themselves.

But you are not helpless. Nor is the parent of any gay child helpless. Nor should you feel isolated or lonely because your child is gay. These are feelings you produce yourself, and only you can deal with them effectively. Unless your distress or your child's is severe, professionals will not help you very much. If emotional disorders are apparent, by all means seek out professional help. If there are no severe emotional problems, then parents can do the job best themselves with the aid of their children.

Most parents don't realize how many resources they have for helping themselves. First of all there are the gay child and his friends. At an earlier point in this book I suggested that you meet your child's friends. This can be a valuable learning experience, especially if some of them are in conflict with their own parents. In most cases you'll find that your child's friends will be willing to talk with you in an honest way about their relationships with their parents. Tactfully encourage such discussions. You'll be amazed how much you can learn from them.

It's also possible for you to meet other parents who have a gay child. Perhaps you can meet the parents of one of your child's friends. Though some people would never agree to such a meeting, others will welcome it. Talking with others who have a gay child is one of the most important things you can do. There is much that you can learn from each other.

The more you speak to helpful people, the more you will alleviate the feeling of loneliness and isolation. If there is a Parents of Gays in your town, go to their meetings; or you can write to the New York chapter. They may be able to give you information about the group nearest your home.

Almost every major city has at least one gay organization. Many of them have separate organizations for gay men and women. Many cities also have gay switchboards. All these organizations are familiar with the needs of gay people, and many of them are sophisticated in answering questions from both gays and their parents. If there is some special group in your area that may be of interest to you, these organizations will know of it. As a rule they are very understanding of the needs and concerns of parents, and they will try to be as helpful as they can. Unfortunately you're unlikely to find their names listed in the Yellow Pages, because the phone companies refuse to list anything under "Gay" or "Homosexual." If you know someone who is gay, you might ask him or her. If there is a college or university in your area, they're likely to have a gay organization. Call the college and ask for information about the group. The college gay group can direct you to others.

You might even try to establish a Parents of Gays group in your own area. Experience has shown that it's not a difficult thing to do, since so many parents feel the need to talk with other parents about homosexuality.

chapter seventeen

THIS CHAPTER
IS FOR GAYS

This book is meant for families, and you are part of a family. If you're gay and reading this book, you care about your family. You're right to care. Unless you're still struggling with conflicting feelings about dependence and independence, you'll want to establish an honest and adult relationship with your family. Perhaps some guidelines will help you.

To begin with, I assume that you are a person who feels comfortable about your homosexuality. If not, most of the information in this chapter is not for you. If you don't understand your own behavior, don't expect your parents to understand it. If you feel inferior or depressed because of your life-style, don't expect your parents to feel good. If you are extremely unhappy with your life, your parents are going to feel unhappy, too.

If you are in need of professional help, get it. Make that the first and most important thing on your list. Don't fidget around deciding whether or not to tell your parents you're gay. That should be discussed with your psychotherapist. If you make this decision without discussing it, you may use your coming out as a weapon and ultimately hurt everyone in your family, including yourself. Get yourself together before you try to tell your parents.

Sometimes talking with other gay people can be more valuable than talking with a professional. Joining a local gay organization, particularly one that is active in the civil rights battle, can be as beneficial as years of therapy. If you are the kind of person who needs to talk and work with other people, then make joining a gay organization your first priority. There's no conflict between seeking professional help and working with other gay people.

Most gays are comfortable with their sexual preference. If you're in this category, you know that psychotherapy for your homosexuality is not necessary. It might even be harmful. But don't be put off if your parents want to seek therapy for you. You need only indicate that it would be unprofitable for you to talk to a psychiatrist, but that you want very much to talk to them. Let's discuss how to talk with your parents.

Begin by recognizing that coming out to your parents is not something you do in one evening. It is a *process* that takes a long time. If your only reason for coming out to them is to give information, don't. It isn't fair to your parents. If you are a responsible person you won't hurt their feelings and then walk out on them.

I know of someone who decided to come out to his parents. He wrote them a *one-paragraph letter* saying he was gay. That's not coming out. It's an attempt to hurt two people by using homosexuality as a weapon. Homosexuality wasn't his problem, but cruelty and lack of maturity. It's not hard to see how dependent this man was on his parents. Why else would he try so hard to hurt them?

If you care about your family, then coming out *begins* the day you disclose your homosexuality. It continues for a long time afterward. During this period you should be ready to talk with your parents whenever they feel the need, and you should be as patient with them as you want them to be with you.

Your parents are going to need a good deal of support. Please provide it. Parents need to know that you are the same son or daughter you were before. They need to know that you love them, and that you care about their feelings. They need to know that you are coming out to them because you don't want to deceive them. Don't assume they know these things. Say them and say them often. Your parents may not hear you clearly at first, but if you persist the message will get through in time.

Time. It takes time. Don't rush them. Some of you needed quite a bit of time to adjust to the idea of being gay. Why should it take your parents less time? Don't push them too hard and expect them to understand quickly. Don't pressure them into saying that they understand when they don't. Understanding usually will come with the passage of time; you can't rush it. And suppose they never understand? That isn't a tragedy either. What is important is that *you* understand and accept what you are doing, and that you can convey to your parents that you do.

Some gays find it useful to practice coming out. They sit down with a friend or two, who act the parts of the parents. Friends can give you feedback about how you sound, and suggestions for doing a better job of it. Friends can be very helpful in this way. They can also share their experiences in coming out to their own parents. Learn about their mistakes, so that you need not repeat them. The good thing about practicing, first, is that you can learn positive ways to come out. No one but your friends will see the errors. In fact, your friends will probably be much tougher than your parents, and if you can satisfy them, you'll probably do a good job with your parents. You're going to be nervous the day you speak to your parents. That's understandable and perfectly normal. People will always be nervous when they're about to do something as important as this. Don't worry about the nervousness, but take some precautions so that it doesn't become overwhelming. When nervousness gets too severe it interferes with honest discussion. Sometimes it leads to conflict. Here are some ways to decrease the anxiety.

Choose the time you'll tell them about your homosexuality. Make it a time when you can be alone with your parents—*without interruption.* Get away from the telephone. Get away from noise in the streets. Get away from little brothers and sisters demanding attention. If you need to, get out of the house. Remember that this should be a private conversation between you and your parents, and that they will need to give you their undivided attention. It will be very difficult for them to handle their own feelings, talk to you, and deal with interruptions as well. Make it your responsibility to set things up right. But even with the best of plans, there may be some distractions. Don't worry about these. Don't let little things get you angry—it will confuse your parents.

It's also helpful to talk with them on a day when things are going well in the family. People hear best when they're feeling their best. If there is trouble in the family, wait until it is resolved. Don't rush to tell your father about your homosexuality right after you've found out that he may not be able to make the mortgage payment. If you've practiced coming out with your friends, and you've set the scene perfectly—and then, just when you're about to talk to your parents they have a fight—wait. It's not the time. There's no rush. You help your parents by choosing the right time and setting, not by telling them quickly. It will not hurt to wait a few more days.

But suppose you choose the right time and the right setting, and they react badly. Perhaps they get angry. What should you do? Parents react with anger or moody silence when they feel hurt. The news of your homosexuality may hurt them, even though you might not have said anything meant to hurt them. Please don't respond to anger with anger. If they hurt your feelings, don't try to hurt back. Try to respond to their hurt feelings, not their attack on you. In most cases this will cause an immediate change in your parents' tone. And even if it doesn't, remember that this is only the first step in a long process. If you do not strike back, your parents may realize how unfair they were and listen more carefully the next time. If you attack them, they will be distracted from thinking about *their unfairness* because they will be thinking about your attack. This is not an easy task for you, but keep in mind that it isn't any easier for them.

Another mistake some people make is confusing their homosexuality with other family issues. This is likely to occur if you get angry, or if one of your parents gets angry. Don't bring up old jealousies or resentments you have against your parents. These will only confuse the issue. Stay with the present. This is not the time to "straighten out" the past. Forget the past right now. Nor should you be distracted by any old wounds they bring up. Certainly don't ever get on the side of one parent against the other.

How much should you tell your parents about your life on the first day? Probably not very much. But that's not because you should be unwilling to tell them. Your major responsibility on the first day is to tell them that you are gay, why you are telling them, and how you feel about them. If you can get this across to them in one day, you've done a remarkable job. You've provided support for them. Information about homosexuality and about your life in particular will come out in later discussions.

Later you can let your parents know how you live. They care very much about this. These also want to

know what kind of friends you have. If there's any reason
to hide this information, perhaps you had better think
about who your friends are! *If they are ready*, let your
parents meet your friends and talk with them. Let your
friends know about this ahead of time, just in case they
don't want to meet your parents. Don't deceive anyone.
Perhaps your parents would like to go to some places
where gays gather. If this is appropriate, encourage them
to do it. Don't try to force them to go, or embarrass them
into going. That will make your parents too nervous, and
nervousness distorts perception. They won't see things
objectively.

*Give your parents as much information about
homosexuality as they want to know, not as much as you
want them to know.* And let them have this information
when they ask for it, not when you want them to have it.
They need to understand your sexual preference in their
own way and in their own time. You should be willing to
work toward their objectives—they need not meet yours.

If your parents want to read more about homosexuality, encourage them to do so. If your city has a gay
book store, you might suggest that all of you browse there
together and choose some books to read. Read them
yourself, as well. Make it a learning experience for all of
you. I am quite certain you will find that some of these
books can teach you a great deal about other gay people.
Discussions centered around the information in the
books can be of great value. If there are no gay book
stores in your area, send for books by mail. There is an
annotated bibliography in the back of this book. Choose
a couple of books (don't buy too many at one time) and
give them to your parents.

How about sex? Should you discuss your sex life
with your parents? Parents rarely ask specific questions
about their children's sex life. Most parents respect the
right to privacy in the matter of sex. In fact, parents I

have talked to have never been concerned with their children's specific sexual experiences. If you feel that your sex life is private, and they ask you about it, you need only express your need for privacy. They will accept it.

Some parents need an unusual amount of time to come to terms with a child's homosexuality. Such parents may react to your coming out with depression or anger. Even though it is difficult, you need to be extra patient with them. Though they may lose their tempers with you, even after they've known for quite a while, you should try not to lose yours. If your parents react so negatively to your homosexuality, and lose sight of you as a son or daughter, it means that the news has hurt them very deeply. In all probability, as in some of the case histories studied earlier, it has stirred emotion-laden areas in themselves. In fact, it may have nothing to do with you. Try not to make things more difficult for them.

It may be very hard for you not to want to hurt them back, but please try. This doesn't mean that you should allow yourself to be abused by your parents because of their own troubles. It may be necessary for you to assert your independence at such a time, and if that is the case, then you must do so. It need not be done with anger or bitterness. Your parents may change their minds. They may come to the realization that they have acted immaturely toward their own child. If they do, they will make amends. But if you respond to anger with anger, you will have cooperated in closing the door to productive family relationships. I believe that the possibility of improvement in the future is worth swallowing some pride in present. I hope you agree.

Under the most extreme circumstances, a child may need to leave the house and move to another area. (Obviously this should be done only by someone who is mature enough to care for himself or herself.) But even if this happens, the door should not be closed forever. If your parents want to visit, you should welcome them as if no problem existed. They may want to correct their errors. If they do, let them. If they do not, you will have no choice but to insist that you direct your own life.

Let me also caution you against another common error that children make when coming out to their parents. Some children want to tell their parents about their homosexuality *because* they want their parents' approval of them and of their sexual preference. This is a serious error, and your parents are likely to pick it up and mention it. If you are an adult, your parents cannot dictate something so important as your sexual and social life-style. Only you can approve or disapprove of it. If you need your parents' approval for what you do, then you have not made a mature, independent decision. The problem is yours, not theirs.

Finally, I want to discuss my reasons for leaving some important information out of this book. You may already have noticed the omission of topics that you feel are important. These omissions are deliberate.

This will be the first reading material most parents have about their child's homosexuality. It is the first that a professional has written extensively for the whole family. My purpose has been to provide a way for you and your parents to talk together and learn from one another. This is my way of helping you share your life with people you love.

Perhaps you would like to have read a discussion of some of the misconceptions that the heterosexual world has about homosexuality: that gays only care about sex, that gay relationships can't last, or that gays prey on immature children. These myths about gay life do not contain even a grain of truth.

Nor have I talked about the kind of caring that can go into a gay relationship. Most parents do not believe that this love can exist. They think that sex is the only thing that holds gay people together. Why haven't I written more about this?

Because it's your job. Parents are not interested in whether *gay people* are happy. Your parents want to know if *you* are happy. They don't care if *gays* are promiscuous, but they care if *you* are. Your parents care about you, and the kind of information they want, only you can give them.

My purpose has been to help provide the right atmosphere for you and your family to talk together. I hope I have been successful. The rest is up to you.

There are a number of good books that parents can read about the lives and experiences of gay people. Some of them are listed in this section. You will notice that the copyright dates are quite recent. There's a good reason why.

Through most of this century gay people could not publish accounts of their lives, fictional or scholarly, unless the information was negative and gay people were depicted as unhappy. In most of the fictional works, publishers insisted that the main gay characters end their lives in suicide. Academic writers found publishers adamant in their refusal to publish anything that contradicted the medical theories of homosexuality as sickness.

It was only in the current decade, with the rise of the gay liberation movement, that more accurate accounts of gay life began to be published. Many have appeared, and many more are in press at this time. Parents will have to be on the lookout for these new books, as some of them will probably be worthwhile reading.

Some of the books listed below will not be found in your local book store or library. However, they are bound to be carried in a gay book shop, and almost every large city in the country has one. If you don't know where the nearest gay book shop can be found, get in touch with a local gay organization. They can direct you.

After You're Out, edited by Karla Jay and Allen Young. Links Books, New York, 1975.
　　This is an anthology spanning a wide and diverse range of issues of concern to gay people. While the articles are not well edited, the book will give the reader a good idea of the lives of gay people.

Christian Sexuality, by Richard R. Mickley. The Universal Fellowship Press, Los Angelos, 1976. $3.95.
　　This book is published by the Metropolitan Community Church,

a church for gay people in many cities of the United States. Primarily expressing Protestant values, the book is a discussion of the relationship between sex and religion.

The Church and the Homosexual, by John J. McNeil, S.J. Sheed Andrews and McMeel, Inc., Kansas City, 1976. $10.
Written by a Jesuit priest, this is a discussion of the Biblical injunctions against homosexual behavior and an analysis of the interpretations of them. The book is well written and readable. It will be of obvious interest to anyone who is concerned about the moral implications of homosexuality.

Consenting Adult, by Laura Z. Hobson. Warner Books, Inc., New York, 1976. Paper.
This is a novelistic account of a mother's discovery that her son is gay. Written by a well-known author, the book illustrates many of the things a parent can do to make matters worse. It is best read with that in mind.

Counseling Parents of Gays, by Rev. Paul H. Shanley. Ampro Inc., 101 Tremont, Boston, Mass. 02108. Audio Cassette, 45 minutes. $7.95.
This Catholic priest was assigned to a ministry to the gay community in Boston. Here he addresses himself directly to Catholic parents. He reviews information about homosexuality, and discusses how parents can avoid negative reactions toward their gay child and why some people are prejudiced against gay people.

The Early Homosexual Rights Movement (1864–1935), by John Lauritsen and David Thorstad. Times Change Press, New York, 1974.
This short but interesting book traces the history of the homophile movement in Germany from the last century to the present day. Informative and relaxed in style, it is highly recommended for those who want to know more about the history of the gay liberation movement.

Familiar Faces, Familiar Lives, by Howard Brown, M.D. Harcourt Brace Jovanovich, New York and London, 1976. $8.95.
This is an important new book by a man who spent most of his professional life keeping his homosexuality a secret. He gives an

account of that life and the changes that occurred when, in middle age, he came out and began to work actively with the gay liberation movement. A poignant book, and highly readable.

The Gay Mystique, by Peter Tisher. Stein and Day, New York, 1973. Paper, $2.95.
    A good introduction to the lives of gay people, written by a man who worked actively in the beginnings of the gay liberation movement. The book discusses at length how gay people live and relate to each other, the effects of the "sickness" label, and attitudes toward gay teachers. Well-written.

Homosexual Behavior Among Males: A Cross-Cultural Approach, by Wainwright Churchill. Prentice-Hall, Inc., Englewood Cliffs, N.J., 1967. Paper, $2.45.
    This is one of the most important books to appear in the past ten years. It examines homosexual behavior in various societies, and discusses the implications of sexual restrictions. The author's theories about sexuality in society have led to some very interesting research by psychologists since the book's publication. More technical than most of the books on this list, but a must for the serious reader.

The Homosexual Dialectic, edited by Joseph A. McCaffrey. Prentice-Hall, Inc., Englewood Cliffs, N.J., 1972.
    Though only a few years old, this is one of the first anthologies about gay people and the gay liberation movement. It is still probably the best one available. The scope of the articles is very broad, and some of them are now considered classics in the history of the gay liberation movement. This book is a must for anyone who wants to understand how gay people perceive the world around them.

Homosexuality, by D. J. West. Aldine Publishing Co., Chicago, 1967.
    This is one of the classic books about homosexuality. It discusses the various forms of homosexual behavior, legal and social issues, psychological and treatment factors. A good resource book.

Homosexuality and the Western Christian Tradition, by Derrick Sherwin Bailey. Archon Books, Hamden, Conn., 1975. First published in 1955 by Longmans, Green & Co., Ltd., London. Reprinted with permission, 1975, in an unaltered and unabridged edition as an Archon Book, an imprint of The Shoe String Press, Inc., Hamden, Conn. 06514.

In a very readable style, this book reviews the Biblical prohibitions against homosexuality and discusses the possible interpretations of passages that are most often cited about homosexual behavior. Recommended for those who are knowledgeable of the Bible and interested in alternative interpretations.

The Lesbian Myth, by Bettie Wysor. Random House, New York, 1974.
This readable book discusses the life of the lesbian in modern society, as well as the various institutions that have opposed lesbian life-styles. The author considers the influences of the church, psychiatry, and the gay liberation movement. There is a very interesting verbatim record of a group of lesbian mothers discussing their lives.

Lesbian/Woman, by Del Martin and Phyllis Lyon, Bantam, New York, 1972.
This book speaks from within the lesbian experience, and this perspective gives it a warmth and reality that cannot be obtained in any other way. They provide a valuable historical view of the internal struggles of the gay liberation movement. Highly recommended.

The Manufacture of Madness, by Thomas S. Szasz. A Delta Book, 1970. Paper.
As one of the most significant psychiatrists in the country today, Szasz gives a comprehensive overview showing how homosexuality was transformed from a social evil to a medical illness. It is probably the finest and most cogent statement of its kind ever written, and highly recommended for all parents.

Out of the Closets: The Sociology of Homosexual Liberation, by Laud Humphreys. Prentice-Hall, Inc., Englewood Cliffs, N.J., 1972.
Written by a sociologist who has been concerned for many years with issues relating to homosexuality, this book looks at the development of the gay liberation movement. The author discusses the stigma of homosexuality and how it has influenced the growth of gay groups, and how the movement has affected gay people. The writing style is easy and relaxed.

Phallos: A Symbol and Its History in the Male World, by Thorkil Vanggaard. International Universities Press, Inc., New York, 1972. Paper.
This remarkable book examines the historical development of male sexual relations, particularly in ancient times. Written with great

clarity, it discusses the system of pederasty that existed in ancient Greece and traces many of our current sexual values to ancient concepts of masculinity and power. A must for serious readers.

The Punishment Cure, by Stephen J. Sansweet. Mason/Charter, New York, 1975.
This book was written by a journalist who investigated the use of cruel forms of treatment in many of our public institutions. The information is likely to be shocking to the average reader, who may be unaware that such abuses take place. It shows quite clearly why gays are so angry at the idea of psychiatric treatment.

The Rights of Gay People: The Basic ACLU Guide to a Gay Person's Rights, by E. Carrington Boggan, Marilyn G. Haft, Charles Lister, and John P. Rupp. Sunrise Books, New York, 1975.

This book is a summary of an ACLU project survey of the legal rights of gay people in the United States today. It discusses the legal issues that concern gay people most, such as lesbian mothers, prison sentences and employment. It gives a good account of the problems of legal discrimination that gay people still face.

Sappho Was a Right-On Woman, by Sidney Abbott and Barbara Love. Stein & Day, New York, 1972.
This book relates the personal experiences of two lesbian women who worked in both the women's movement and the gay liberation movement. Dealing with their lives as lesbians and the problems of discrimination, it is the best book of its kind. Highly recommended.

Society and the Healthy Homosexual, by George Weinberg. Anchor Books, Doubleday & Company, Garden City, N.Y., 1973. Paper.
Weinberg begins by considering the psychological implications of homophobia, the irrational fear of gay people, and goes on to discuss the value of psychotherapy for gays. There is an interesting chapter for parents of a gay child. A readable book.